*

>Khushal Khan Khattak<

The Great Warrior-Poet
of
Afghanistan

*

~Selected Poetry~

A Selection by the same Author
(See back pages of this book for descriptions of some)

TRANSLATIONS: Divan of Hafiz, Hafiz: The Oracle, Ruba'iyat of Hafiz, Hafiz: Tongue of the Hidden, Hafiz: Book of the Winebringer, Hafiz: Love's Perfect Gift, Hafiz: Selected Poems, Seven Hundred Sayings of Kabir, Ruba'iyat of Rumi, Ruba'iyat of Sadi, Rumi: Selected Poems, Divan of Sadi, Nizami: Layla and Majnun, Nizami: Treasury of the Mysteries, Nizami: Selected Poems, Obeyd Zakani: The Dervish Joker, Obeyd Zakani's Mouse & Cat, Hafiz's Friend: Jahan Khatun, Piercing Pearls: The Complete Anthology of Persian Poetry (2 vols.); Princesses, Sufis, Dervishes, Martyrs and Feminists: Eight Women Poets of the East, Makhfi: The Princess Sufi Poet Zeb-un-Nissa, The Sufi Ruba'iyat: An Anthology, The Sufi & Dervish Ghazal: An Anthology, The Ruba'iyat: A World Anthology, The Ghazal: A World Anthology, The Divine Wine: A Treasury of Sufi & Dervish Poetry (2 vols.), The Masnavi: A World Anthology, The Qasida: A World Anthology, Ibn Al-Farid: Wine & The Mystic's Progress, Unity in Diversity: Anthology of Sufi Poets of Indian Sub-Continent; Tongues on Fire: Anthology of the Poets of Afghanistan; Wine, Blood & Roses: Anthology of Turkish Poets, Love's Agony & Bliss: Anthology of Urdu Poetry; Hearts With Wings: Anthology of Persian Sufi & Dervish Poetry, Breezes of Truth: Selected Arabic Sufi Poetry, Yunus Emre, Turkish Dervish: Selected Poems, Anthology of Classical Arabic Poetry, The Qit'a: Anthology of the 'Fragment' in Arabic, Persian & Eastern Poetry, Ruba'iyat of al-Ma'arri, Ruba'iyat of Sarmad, Ruba'iyat of 'Attar, Ruba'iyat of Abu Said, Ruba'iyat of Mahsati, Ruba'iyat of Baba Tahir, Ruba'iyat of Jahan Khatun, Ruba'iyat of Sana'i, Sana'i: Selected Poems, The Poets of Shiraz, Ruba'iyat of Jami, Jami: Selected Poems, Ruba'iyat of Khayyam, Ruba'iyat of Auhad ud-din, Huma: Selected Poems of Meher Baba, Rudaki: Selected Poems, The Seven Golden Odes (Qasidas) of Arabia, The Qita: Anthology of 'Fragment' in Arabic, Persian and Eastern Poetry, Ruba'iyat of Nesimi, Nesimi: Selected Poems, Ruba'iyat of Bedil, Bedil: Selected Poems, Anvari: Selected Poems, Ruba'iyat of 'Iraqi, The Wisdom of Ibn Yamin, Shabistari: The Rose Garden of Mystery, Shimmering Jewels: Anthology of Poetry under the Mughal Emperors of India (1526-1857), Amir Khusrau: Selected Poems, Rahman Baba: Selected Poems, Ruba'iyat of Dara Shikoh, Ruba'iyat of Ansari, Poems of Majnun (Qays), Mu'in ud-din Chishti: Selected Poems, Anthology of Poets of the Chishti Sufi Order, A Wealth of Poets: Persian Poetry at the Courts of Sultan Mahmud in Ghazneh & Sultan Sanjar in Ghanjeh (998-1158), Shah Ni'matullah Vali: Selected Poems, Ruba'iyat of Ni'matullah, Poets of the Ni'matullah Sufi Order, Ansari: Selected Poems, Baba Farid: Selected Poems., Qasidah Burdah: The Three Poems of the Prophet's Mantle, 'Iraqi: Selected Poems, 'Attar: Selected Poems, Ruba'iyat of Anvari, 'Iraqi: Selected Poems, Zarathustra: Selected Poems, Khushal Khan Khattak: The Great Warrior & Poet of Afghanistan, Mansur Hallaj: Selected Poems, Ruba'iyat of Baba Afzal.

FICTION: Hafiz of Shiraz: A Novel-Biography (3 vols), The First Mystery, The Second Mystery, Hafiz: The Ugly Little Boy Who Became a Great Poet, Pan of the Never-Never, The Greatest Game, The Healer and the Emperor, Golf is Murder, The Zen Golf Murder, Riana, The Greatest Game, Going Back.

POETRY: Pune: The City of God, Cradle Mountain, Pie Anthology (Editor); The Master, The Muse & The Poet: An Autobiography in Poetry; A Bird in His Hand, Compassionate Rose, The Cross of God.

SCREENPLAYS: Hafiz of Shiraz, Layla & Majnun, Riana, The Castlemaine Kiss, The Greatest Game, The Healer & The Emperor, Golf is Murder, The Zen-Golf Murder, Pan of The Never-Never, Going Back. STAGE: Hafiz of Shiraz, Hafiz: The Musical.

RADIO: The Sun of Shiraz. DANCE: The Eternal Triangle (with Meher Baba).

TELEVISION: The Mark, The First Mystery, Pan of The Never-Never, Hafiz: The Series.

★

>Khushal Khan Khattak<

The Great Warrior-Poet of Afghanistan

★

~Selected Poetry~

Translations and Introduction

Paul Smith

NEW HUMANITY BOOKS

BOOK HEAVEN
Booksellers & Publishers

Copyright © Paul Smith 2012.

NEW HUMANITY BOOKS

BOOK HEAVEN
(Booksellers & Publishers for over 40 years)
47 Main Road
Campbells Creek, Victoria 3451
Australia

newhumanitybooks@hotmail.com

ISBN: 978-1479397808

Poetry/Mysticism/Sufism/Afghan Studies/
Pashtu Literature

CONTENTS

The Life, Times & Poetry
of
Khushal Khan Khattak ... page 7

Selected Bibliography... 21

The Various Forms of Poetry used by Khushal... 22

Ruba'is... 37

Ghazals... 57

Qasidas... 153

Qit'as... 165

Masnavi... 181

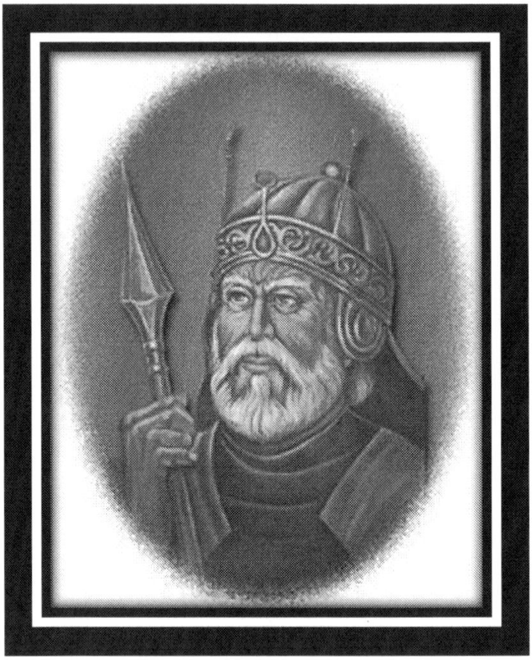

THE LIFE, TIMES & POETRY OF KHUSHAL KHAN KHATTAK

Khushal Khan Khattak (1613-1689) was a prominent Pashtun poet, warrior, a charismatic personality and tribal chief of the Khattak tribe. He wrote a huge collection of Pashtu poems during the Mughal Empire in the 17th century and admonished Pashtuns to forsake their divisive tendencies and unite against the Mughal Army.

Promoting Pashtun nationalism through poetry, Khushal Khan Khattak is the first Afghan mentor who presents his theories for the unity of the Afghan resistance against the foreign parts and the creation of a nation-state. His life was spent in struggling against the oppressive Mughal governments of India. In order to restore Afghan freedom Khushal Khan challenged Emperor Aurangzeb's powers. He defeated the Mughal troops in many engagements. The stand and fight of Khushal Khan Khattak is an important part of Afghan history.

His thoughts form the basis of the political and literary movements in Afghanistan. The opinions and ideas of Khushal Khan Khattak form a new stage in the ideological and intellectual development of the Afghans. What he has done for his language and his people is unprecedented in the cultural development of the Afghans.

His theories and thesis correspond to those of many of large thinkers of the world and he can be considered an international personality. He also has written in Persian and Hindi. He was a renowned military fighter who became known as an Afghan warrior-poet.

Western scholars regard Khushal Khan Khattak as a national hero and poet of Afghanistan. He lived in the foothills of the Hindu Kush mountains in what is now Khyber Pakhtunkhwa in Pakistan.

He was born about 1613 into the Khattak tribe. He was the son of Malik Shahbaz Khan Khattak from Akora, Mughal ruled India (now in Nowshera District of Kyber-Pakthunkhwa, in Pakistan). His grandfather, Malik Akoray, was the first Khattak to enjoy widespread fame during the reign of the Mughal emperor Jalal-ud-din Akbar.

Akoray moved from Teri (a village in Karak District) to Sarai Akora, the town that Akoray founded and built. Akoray cooperated with the Mughals to safeguard the trunk route and was generously rewarded for his assistance. The Akor Khels, a clan named after Akoray, still hold a prominent position in the Khattak tribe. The Khattak tribe of Khushal Khan now lives in areas of Karak, Kohat, Nowshera, Cherat, Peshawar, Mardan and in other parts of the Khyber Pakhtunkhwa.

Khushal Khan's life can be divided into two important parts... during his adult life he was mostly engaged in the service of the Mughal emperor, and during his old age he was preoccupied with the idea of the unification of the Pashtuns.

He was an intelligent and bold person from childhood. His first involvement in war occurred when he was just 13 years old. Apart from the fact that he was a scholar, thinker, philosopher and great poet he was a prince and leaders of his tribe simultaneously. His forefathers were since the 16th century officers of the Mughal Empire.

Khushal Khan received his early education at home. In those days the formal system of education did not exist. Therefore, the rich and prosperous people used to hire teachers to teach their children at home. His father was also economically prosperous because he was on a prominent position in the Mughal army. Moreover the Mughal emperor Shah Jahan had given a lot of land to his father, due to which he could easily afford the educational expenses of his son. Therefore, he also hired the services of some teachers to teach his son at home. One was Maulana Abdul Hakeem and the other was Awais Multani. In a poem, he praised Maulana Abdul Hakeem with the following words. "Maulana Abdul Hakeem is a physician of religious and worldly knowledge. He did respect even Hindu ascetics. Someone made objection to this but he replied, 'you do not understand.... good treatment with everyone is *Sirat-e-Mustaqeem* (straight way or path of religion)'".

He was very fond of hunting and swordplay. In this regard, it seems that he had a stronger bent for hunting than education. As he, himself says in the following couplet: "Knowledge of the world would have been mine, had I not indulged in the hobby of hunting".

After the death of his father Shahbaz Khan, Emperor Shah Jahan appointed him as the tribal chief and Mansabdar in 1641 at the age of 28. After the death of Shah Jahan tension was created with Aurangzeb. Aurangzeb arrested Khushal Khan Khattak. In 1658, Aurangzeb, Shah Jahan's successor, threw him into prison in the Gwalior fortress. When he returned, he dissociated himself from the Mughal Empire slowly and started with resistance later. He contacted other Pashtun tribes and with support of his people he started a systematic resistance against the Mughals.

After he was permitted to return to Pashtun dominated areas (Eastern Afghanistan and western Pakistan), Khushal had been shocked by the unfriendly treatment he received from

Mughal authorities and Emperor Aurangzeb whose indifference and coolness towards his plight had wounded Khushal's ego. He used to say, "I had done nothing wrong against the interests of the king or the empire". Mughal authorities continued to offer him temptations in order to reclaim him to their service but Khushal resisted all such offers and made it clear to the Mughals that "I served your cause to the best of my honesty, I subdued and killed my own Pashtuns to promote the Empire's interests but my services and my loyalty did not make me a Mughal". According to Khushal, he was burning inside to exact revenge, but preferred to keep silent. Nevertheless the Mughals were not inclined to bear his aloofness and therefore he was challenged either "to be friend or foe" as the interests of empire knew no impartiality.

Khushal decided to be a foe and joined Darya Khan Afridi and Aimal Khan Mohmand in their fight and wars against Mughals. He dissociated himself from the Mughal Empire and he incited the Afghan tribes to rebel against Aurangzeb. In the Mughal Empire the Pashtun tribesmen were considered the bedrock of the Mughal army. They were the Empire's bulwark from the threat in the North-West as well as the main fighting force against the Sikhs and Marathas. The Pashtun revolt occurred in 1672 under the leadership Khushal. The revolt was triggered when soldiers under the orders of the Mughal Governor Amir Khan allegedly attempted to molest women of the Safi tribe in modern day Kunar. The Safi tribe retaliated and killed the soldier. This attack provoked a reprisal, which triggered a general revolt of the most of tribes. The Mughal emperor Aurangzeb ordered the Safi tribal elders to hand over the killers. The Safi, Afridi, Mohmand, Shinwari and Khattak tribes came together to protect the Safi men accused. Attempting to reassert his authority, Amir Khan in orders of Aurangzeb led a large Mughal army to the Khyber Pass, where the army was surrounded by tribesmen and routed.

Afghan sources claim that Aurangzeb suffered a humiliating defeat, with a reported loss of 40,000 soldiers and with only four men, including the Governor managing to escape. In a battle Khushal lost his friends Emal Khan Mohmand and Darya Khan Afridi. Khushal greatly praised the bravery and courage of Darya Khan Afridi and Aimal Khan Mohmad who had destroyed the entire Mughal army in Khyber in 1672. As he said about his these two close companions: "Aimal Khan and Darya Khan from death God preserve them, never have they failed me at the time of need".

After that the revolt spread, with the Mughals suffering a near total collapse of their authority along the Pashtun belt.

The closure of the important Attock-to-Kabul trade route along the Grand Trunk road was particularly critical. By 1674, the situation had deteriorated to a point where Aurangzeb himself camped at Attock to personally take charge. Switching to diplomacy and bribery along with force of arms, the Mughals eventually split the rebellion and while they never managed to wield effective authority outside the main trade route, the revolt was partially suppressed. However, the long term anarchy on the Mughal frontier that prevailed as a consequence ensured that Nadir Shah's Khorasanian forces half a century later faced little resistance on the road to Delhi.

Khushal continued to resist the Mughals on war fronts. These wars according to historians shook the foundations of the Mughal Empire. Khushal gave a romantic touch with his poetry to his nationalist ideology, he visited the far flung areas, met with Pashtun tribal chiefs, particularly the Yousafzais, negotiated with them to bring about unity in Pashtun ranks against Mughals but failed in his efforts and returned broken-hearted.

After failing to unite the Pashtun tribes Khushal Khan retired as a warrior and used his pen to point to weaknesses of his society, he was not only a great warrior but had keen sense wordplay.

Khushal Khan Khatak wrote thousands of poems mostly patriotic about his roots, about his tribe, about his nation and triumphs over invaders.

Upon his retirement, his many sons began fighting for leadership. Meanwhile the Mughals had bribed his son Behram Khan to arrest or to kill Khushal. About this, Khushal says, "My one demerit devours all my merits that I am Behram's father and Behram is my son".

Behram then sent his men to arrest his father. Upon the army's advance, Khushal Khan at the age of 77 suited up in his armour, along with his only two brave sons, Nusrat Khan and Gohar Khan (only those two sons accompanied him until his death) and drew his sword and called out; "Whoever are men among you, come to this sword if you dare." The men returned to Bahram in shame. Bahram joined forces with the Mughals set to capture his father and before he could do so, Khushal fled into Afridi territory assisted by his two sons Nusrat Khan and Gohar Khan.

Khushal Khan passed away at the age of 78 on Friday, the 20th February 1689 at Dambara, after attempting for so many years to unite the various Pashtun tribes. It is believed that he had gone on an expedition to 'Tirah', a rugged mountainous area in Khyber Pakhtunkhwa where he died.

People searched for him and found his dead body a number of days later with his sword and the carcass of his horse (known as 'Silai' in Pashtu, which means 'wind'). His death symbolizes his courage and his love for his Afghan motherland.

He desired before his death that he should be buried in a place where the dust of Mughal horses' hoofs may not fall on his grave His wishes were carried out by his friend and his remains were laid at 'Esoori' village in the Akora Khattak in Khattaks hills, where many Pashtuns continue to pay tribute and visit his tomb. His grave carries the inscription: *Da Afghan Pa nang mai watarala toora, nangyalai da zamanai Khushal Khattak Yam.* "I have taken up the sword to defend the pride of the Afghan, I am Khushal Khattak, the honorable man of the age."

Muhammad Iqbal was a famous poet in the subcontinent who came to know about Khushal through translations. He not only highly appreciated his poetry but also developed a great respect for him. Iqbal called him the *Hakim* (philosopher) and *Tabeeb* (physician) of Afghanistan. Iqbal expressed his desire that if he knew Pashtu he would have translated Khushal's poetry into Urdu or Persian. This is really a great tribute to a great man by another great man. Khushal Khan was a practical man. He manifested all those qualities in his living conduct that he wanted to see in a man. Muhammad Iqbal the great philosopher said about Khushal Khan Khattak: "That Afghan *shanas* (Khushal Khan Khattak) said well, he expressed what he saw without any hesitation. He was the Hakeem (Philosopher) of Afghan nation. He was the physician of Afghan cause. He stated the secrets of his nation boldly. He was writing and said the right very wisely."

Khushal lived a life of sometimes misery and affliction, but he never bowed to the Mughals, he never compromised on principles, he remained committed to his ideal that even a poor independence is better than a kingdom. Few men in history better deserve to be acclaimed as national heroes as Khushal. He is not only the Firdausi of the Afghans but he also plays the role of Rustom in Afghan history. Only very few personalities around the world may be a parallel to him. Khushal's critics differ about his greatness: some consider him the greatest with reference to his poetry, some consider him to be the greatest warrior, others confirm him to be the greatest philosopher and statesman and still others consider him the great preacher of love and amity.

He loved humanity, he loved Pashtuns, he loved knowledge and beauty in all its forms whether of mountains, trees flowers, birds and women. He still lives in memory and history. Time never ever seems to be able to lessen his thoughts and vibrant personality.

Khushal wrote excellent poetry in Pashtu about such things as unity, honor, war, love, and everyday life. He also wrote about philosophy and ethics. His poetry is still widely read. Khushal faced the hard life. The victim of old age, the hard life of wars and worries and his head-on collisions with the Mughal imperial power had indeed eroded his strength and energy but his courage, bravery and perseverance was intact. He fathered more than sixty sons and thirty daughters and when not fighting the Mughals or writing books took great pleasure in hunting and falconry.

His poetry consists of more than 45,000 poems! According to some historians, the number of books written by Khattak are more than 200. He is the author of numerous works in Pashtu and Persian, consisting of Poetry, Medicine, Ethics, Religious Jurisprudence, Philosophy, Falconry, Geography of Swat, an account of his own exile and imprisonment, a prose autobiography and family history, a discourse between pen and sword. He even invented a type of shorthand that he called 'chain writing'. His more famous books are *Baz Nama, Fazal Nama, Distar Nama* and *Farrah Nama* and a large *Divan* of *ghazals* and *qasidas* and over 2000 *ruba'is*. There is not another poet in the Afghan language of Pashtu who created so many poems on such a wide range of subjects.

Before him there was one poet who wrote mainly in Pashtu... Mirza Ansari who probably died in 1630. Mirza (his pen-name) Khan Ansari was one of the first poets to help perfect a Pusthu style. He was a predecessor of the great Sufi Poet, Rahman Baba. Mirza was a descendant, probably a grandson of Pir Roshan, the founder of the Roshanian sect that held an uprising among the Afghans in 1542. Kasim Ali Afridi, an Afghan poet of India, in one of his *qasidas* states that Mirza Khan was of Bayzid's family. He held the same beliefs as the Sufis and was a disciple of Mulla Suliman from the town of Jalandhar in the Punjab. Mirza was a great traveller and well known from Herat to Agra. Amazingly the fundamentalist emperor, Aurangzeb, gave him an allowance, but eventually Mirza was summoned by the monarch on accusations of heresy and blasphemy, but the emperor finally saved him. Mirza's poems contain many Arabic and Dari words, but his Pashtu is very ancient, particularly in words used amongst the hill tribes of Eastern Afghanistan. The Sanskrit in Mirza's poems came from the fact of his long residence in India. It is said that Mirza, in the later years of his life, married and settled in the Tirah district to the south of the Khyber Pass.

In Khushal's mystical or Sufi love poems one can strongly feel the influence of Mirza and the great Persian poet Hafiz.

Dost Mohammad Khan Kamil was the first Pashtun scholar to initiate research on Khattak along scientific lines. He wrote two important and comprehensive books, one in English called *On a Foreign Approach to Khushal* and the other in Urdu titled *Khushal Khan Khattak* published in 1952. *Diwan-i-Khushal Khan Khattak* was published under the directive of H .W. Bellew in 1869 (Jail Press, Peshawar), the manuscript of which was provided by Sultan Bakhash Darogha, an employee of the British government. More recently his poetry has been translated again.

In October 2002, a book on Khushal Khan Khattak, *Khushal Khan, The Afghan Warrior Poet and Philosopher*, was published. It was sponsored by Pashtun Cultural Society and Pashto Adabi Society of Islamabad/Rawalpindi. The book is written by a well known writer and scholar, Ghani Khan Khattak, who is reputed for having established the literary and cultural societies, and for promoting Pashto literary and cultural activities in the capital of Pakistan, Islamabad. The significance of the book lies in that this is the first book in

English on the life of Khushal Khan. Most of the written material available on him is either in Pashtu or in Urdu. Although translators and scholars have always given importance to Khattak in their findings but they have not ever presented a detailed life story of Khushal Khan.

Sources:

Wikipedia Article

Selections from the Poetry of the Afghans, from the 16th to the 19th Century by H.G. Raverty, Calcutta, 1862.

SELECTED BIBLIOGRAPHY

Diwan-i-Khushal Khan Khattak, Jail Press, Peshawar, 1869.

Dastar Nams of Khushal Khan Khattak Translated into English by Prof. Arif Naseen, Pashto Achademy, University of Peshawar, 2007.

Selections from the Poetry of the Afghans, from the 16th to the 19th Century by H.G. Raverty, Calcutta, 1862. (Pages 150-250).

Selections from the Poetry of Khushal Khan Khattak, by C. Biddulph, London, 1890.

The Poems of Khushal Khan Khattak by Evelyn Howell & Olaf Caroe, Oxford University Press, Peshawar, 1963.

Poems from the Diwan of Khushal Khan Khattak by Dr. N. Mackenzie, Allen & Unwin, London, 1965.

On a Foreign Approach to Khushal: A Critique of Caroe & Howell, by Dost Mohammad Khan Kamil. Maktabeh-I- Shaheen, Peshawar, 1968.

Khushal Khan, The Afghan Warrior and Philosopher, by Ghani Khan, Pashtoon Cultural Society, Islamabad, 2002.

Afghan Poetry of the Seventeenth Century by C.E. Biddulph, London, 1890.

The Pathans by Sir Olaf Caroe, London, 1958.

Translation of the Kalid-I Afghani by T.C. Plowden, Lahore, 1875.

Khushal Khan: the national poet of the Afghans, G Morgenstierne. Journal of Royal Central Asian Society, 1960.

The Various Forms of Poetry used by Khushal

The Ruba'i

Many scholars of Persian Poetry believe that the *ruba'i* is the most ancient Persian poetic form that is original to this language and they state that all other classical forms including the *ghazal, qasida, masnavi, qit'a* and others originated in Arabic literature and the metres employed in them were in Arabic poetry in the beginning... this, can be disputed.

The Persian language is a fine intercourse of Arabic (a masculine-sounding language) and Pahlavi (feminine-sounding language) that is mainly a descendant of the profound language of the Spiritual Master Zoroaster... Zend. Sanskrit is also a branch of that ancient language[*] (e.g. Zend: *garema* or heat is in Sanskrit *gharma*, in Pahlavi is *garma*, Persian... *garm*) given to us by that prophet whose perfect and profound teachings in the *gathas* of the *Avesta* were composed in a form very close to the *ruba'i* which one might believe could give him the title not only of the founder of the Persian language and people and mysticism... but also of Persian poetry's most individualistic form of poetic expression.

One can trace the origins of this poetical language back

almost 7000 years to Zoroaster's time, not merely less than 2600 years... a mistake that most recent scholars made by confusing the last Zoroastian *priest* bearing his name with that of this original Prophet, the *Rasool* or Messiah, who like Moses, led out his people from their original Aryan lands in Bactria, when they were invaded by many hordes of murderous barbarians.

On that remarkable and in many aspects, far-reaching journey, an argument occurred amongst his people when they had reached what we today call India and many left him and settled there and their language eventually evolved into Sanskrit. Zoroaster then took his remaining followers west and finally settled near Shiraz in Fars, and Zend eventually became Pahlavi and the Aryan language continued west and founded many languages in Europe, including English.

Now as to the origin of the metre of the *ruba'i* I offer two of Zoroaster's poems or *gathas* to enjoy and consider, even though the metre may not be that of the *ruba'i*, the rhyme structure and content are similar.

Wise One, with these short poems I come before You, praising Your Righteousness, deeds of Good Mind too.

And when I arrive at that bliss that has come to me... may these poems of this man of insight... come through.

And another...

May good rulers and not evil ones over us be ruling!
O devoted, by doing good works for mankind, bring
rebirth... prepare all this for what's good for all men:
through work in the field, let ox for us be fattening.

The *ruba'i* is a poem of four lines in which usually the first, second and fourth lines rhyme and sometimes with the *radif* (refrain) after the rhyme words... sometimes all four rhyme. It is composed in metres called *ruba'i* metres. Each *ruba'i* is a separate poem in itself and should not be regarded as a part of a long poem as was created by FitzGerald when he translated those he attributed to Omar Khayyam.

The *ruba'i* (as its name implies) is two couplets *(beyts)* in length, or four lines *(misra)*. The *ruba'i* is a different metre from those used in Arabic poetry that preceded it.

How was this metre invented? The accepted story of Rudaki (d. 941) creating this new *metre* of the *hazaj* group which is essential to the *ruba'i* is as follows: one New Year's Festival *(Nowruz)* he happened to be strolling in a garden where some children played with nuts and one threw a walnut along a groove in a stick and it jumped out then rolled back again creating a sound and the children shouted with delight in imitation, 'Ghaltan ghaltan hami ravad ta bun-i gau,' (Ball,

ball, surprising hills to end of a brave try]. Rudaki immediately recognised in the line's metre a new invention and by the repetition four times of the *rhyme* he had quickly created the *ruba'i*... and is considered the first master of this form and the father of classical Persian Poetry.

Shams-e Qais writing two hundred years later about this moment of poetic history and the effect of this new form on the population said the following... "This new poetic form fascinated all classes, rich and poor, ascetic and drunken rebel-outsider*[rend]*, all wanted to participate in it... the sinful and the good both loved it; those who were so ignorant they couldn't make out the difference between poetry and prose began to dance to it; those with dead hearts who couldn't tell the difference between a donkey braying and reed's wailing and were a thousand miles away from listening to a lute's strumming, offered up their souls for a *ruba'i*. Many young cloistered girls, from passion for the song of a *ruba'i* broke down the doors and their chastity's walls; many matrons from love for a *ruba'i* let loose the braids of their self-restraint."

And so, the *ruba'i* should be eloquent, spontaneous and ingenious. In the *ruba'i* the first three lines serve as an introduction to the fourth that should be sublime, subtle or pithy and clever. As can be seen from the quote by Shams-e

Qais above, the *ruba'i* immediately appealed to all levels of society and has done so ever since. The nobility and royalty enjoyed those in praise of them and the commoner enjoyed the short, simple homilies... the ascetic and mystic could think upon epigrams of deep religious fervour and wisdom; the reprobates enjoyed the subtle and amusing satires and obscenities... and for everyone, especially the cloistered girls and old maids, many erotic and beautiful love poems to satisfy any passionate heart.

Almost every major and minor poet in Persia composed at some time in the *ruba'i* form and the form has been adapted by poets of other languages including Turkish, Urdu and Pashtu... Khushal Khan Khattak writing over 2000 of them, probably the first to do so in that language.

Note: See *'Comparative Grammar, Lecture 6'* in *'Lectures on the Science of Language' 1861* By *Max Muller, Reprint Munshi Ram Manohar Lal, Delhi, 1965.*
The *Encyclopaedia Britannica Volume xxi, Eleventh Edition Cambridge 1911 (Pages 246-8).*

The Ghazal.

There is really no equivalent to the *ghazal* (pronounced *guz'el*) in English poetry although Masud Farzaad,* perhaps the greatest Iranian authority on Hafiz (he spent much his lifetime finding the Variorum Edition) and his *ghazals* says, the sonnet is probably the closest. As a matter of fact, the *ghazal* is a unique form and its origin has been argued about for many centuries.

Some say that the *ghazal* originated in songs that were composed in Persia to be sung at court before Persia was converted to Islam, but not one song has survived to prove this. It is also possible that originally the *ghazals* were songs of love that were sung by minstrels in the early days of Persian history and that this form passed into poetry down the ages. I find this explanation plausible for the following reasons: firstly, the word *ghazal* means 'a conversation between lovers.' Secondly, the *ghazals* of Hafiz, Sadi and others were often put to music and became songs, which have been popular in Persia from ancient times until now.

Other scholars see the *ghazal* as coming from Arabic poetry, especially the prelude to longer poems: they say that this prelude was isolated and changed, to eventually become the *ghazal*. The Arabic root of the word *ghazal* is *gazl* which means: spinning, spun, thread, twist... the form of the *ghazal* is a spiral.

Whatever the origin, by the fourteenth century the *ghazal* had become a mature form of poetry. Among the great *ghazal* writers in Persian of the past were Nizami, Farid ad-Din 'Attar, Rumi and Sadi; but with the *ghazals* of Hafiz and other poets in Shiraz during his lifetime this form reached its summit.

The form of the *ghazal* at first glance seems simple, but on a deeper inspection it will be found that there is more to it than one at first sees.

It is usually between five and fifteen couplets (*beyts* or 'houses'), but sometimes more. A *beyt* is 'a line of verse split into two equal parts scanning exactly alike.' Each couplet has a fixed rhyme which appears at the end of the second line. In the first couplet which is called the *matla* meaning 'orient' or 'rising,' the rhyme appears at the end of both lines. This first couplet has the function of 'setting the stage' or stating the subject matter and feeling of the poem. The other couplets or *beyts* have other names depending on their positions. One could say that the opening couplet is the subject, the following couplets the actions: changing, viewed from different angles, progressing from one point to another, larger and deeper, until the objective of the poem is reached in the last couplet. The final couplet is known as the *maqta* or 'point of section.' This couplet or the one before it almost always contains the *takhallus* or pen-name of the poet, signifying that it was written by him and also allowing him the chance to detach himself from himself and comment on what effect the actions of the subject matter in the preceding couplets had on him. Often the poet uses a play on words when he uses his own pen-name... ('Hafiz' for example, means: a preserver, a guardian, rememberer, watchman, one who knows the *Koran* by heart).

In the *ghazal* the Persian Master Poets found the ideal instrument to express the great tension between the opposites that exist in this world. Having the strict rhyming structure of the same rhyme at the end of the second line of each couplet (after the first couplet) the mind must continually come back to the world and the poem and the rhyme. But by being allowed to use any word at the end of the first line of each couplet, one can be as spontaneous as possible and give the heart its full rein. This of course happens also in the first line of the first couplet, for whatever word or rhyme-sound that comes out in the first line sets the rhyme for the rest of the *ghazal*. So the 'feeling' created by the rhyme is one that comes spontaneously from the heart, and this spontaneity is allowed to be expanded from then on in the non-rhyming lines, and to contract in those lines that rhyme, when the mind must function as an 'orderer' of the poem. This expansion and contraction, feeling and thinking, heart and mind, combine to produce great tension and power that spirals inward and outward and creates an atmosphere that I would define as 'deep nostalgia.' This deep nostalgia is a primal moving force that flows through all life, art and song, and produces within whoever comes into contact with it when it is consciously expressed, an irresistible yearning to unite the opposites that it contains. In the *ghazal* any metre can be employed except the *ruba'i* metre.

The true meaning of Sufism, apart from the recognition of God in human form as the *Qutub* or the *Rasool* or the Christ is *tassawuf*... that means to get to the essence of everything. Adam was the first poet and it is said that he named everything and invented the first alphabet from which all others come. But Adam was not only the creator of conscious language as we know it, he was also the creator of song and the perfect form through which he created songs in praise of Eve his true Beloved, her beauty was displayed in the spiral form of the *ghazal*. So, the *ghazals* he composed and sung to her before their eventual Spiritual Union were of longing and separation and those after... of the bliss of Union. He used the same form of song about other events including the great sorrow and deep nostalgia about the loss of his favourite son Abel.

Two of Arabia's most careful and serious historians Tabari (d.923) and Masudi (d.957) state that the first poem ever composed in known history was one by Adam on the death of Abel and the form was the *ghazal*.

The lands are changed and all those who live upon them,
the face of the earth is torn and surrounded with gloom;
everything that was lovely and fragrant has now faded,
from that beautiful face has vanished the joyful bloom.
What deep regrets for my dear son... O regrets for Abel,
a victim of murder... who has been placed into the tomb!
Is it possible to rest, while that Devil that was cursed
who never fails or dies... up from behind us does loom?
"Give up these lands and all of those who live on them;
I was the one who forced you out of Paradise, your room,
where you and your wife were so secure and established,
where your heart did not know of the world's dark doom!
But you, you did escape all of my traps and my trickery,
until that great gift of life... upon which you did presume
you went and lost... and from Aden the blasts of wind,
but for God's Grace, would've swept you like a broom!"

It is said that thousands of years after Adam, the Perfect Spiritual Master Noah, settled Shiraz after his ark landed in the Turkish lands on the mountains of Ararat and was a vintner who brought the first vines that he carried with him was also a poet who composed in this form as did the *Qutub* of some three thousand years later who also settled his people he had led from their homeland in Bactria (northern Afghanistan) to Fars (Persia)... Zoroaster.

His *gathas* or hymns are in rhyme-structure the first two couplets of the *ghazal* that would later be known as the *ruba'i*. And so the *ghazals* of the Zoroastrians were sung in their winehouses and fire temples throughout our land until the Muslim Arabs invaded and converted most to Islam, but poets and minstrels would not give up their much loved eternal God-given *ghazal* or the wine of Noah as well, which had its distant progeny in the *mesqali* grape.

The clandestine winehouses run by the Zoroastrians and Christians became the venues for many hundreds of years of the *ghazal*. In these winehouses Persians could criticise their Arab and Turkish rulers and their police chiefs and false Sufi masters and hypocritical clergy who censored and forbade them to practice the drinking of wine and the appreciation of beautiful faces and forms of unveiled women and handsome young men. In the winehouses the truth could be told and this truth was quickly spread by the minstrels in the market places and even at court through what was becoming a popular form of expression amongst the masses. And although in fact the actual drinking of wine finally became less because of the religious restrictions, it as a symbol of truth, love and freedom became more widespread.

Of course there always existed another 'Winehouse' where the Wine of Divine Love and Grace was poured out by the Winebringer or *Qutub,* the Perfect Master or the Old Magian. Here the wine and truth that flowed freely from heart to heart was of the spiritual nature and made the lover or drunkard so intoxicated with the Divine Beloved that he became *mast-*like... mad with longing to be united with the Eternal One, Whose beauty he saw and appreciated in the face and form and personality of his earthly beloved whom he praised, wooed, begged, cajoled, described, desired and desperately longed for through his *ghazals* and by his actions and with each breath of his whole life he came closer to the Eternal Beloved. Human love became transmuted into Divine Love. Hafiz's love for Shakh-e Nabat is an example of this.

Although the poets of the *ghazal* may appear to many as open-minded, drunken, outcast lovers, it does not necessarily mean that they all drank the juice of the grape... for it is an inner state that they often were expressing. The *ghazal* is a conversation between the lover and the beloved and as in all intimate conversation... the talk flows both ways. The subject may not necessary be about love, but it is always from the point of view of one who loves truth, love and beauty.

The first to compose in this form in Pashtu (that we know of) was the Sufi poet Mirza Khan, followed by Khushal Khan Khattak, who wrote many thousands of them.

*Hafeez and his Poems by Masud Farzaad. Stephen Austin & Sons Ltd. Hertford, 1949.

The Qasida

This kind of poem resembles a *ghazal* in many ways except that it is longer than the *ghazal* and is often as long as a hundred couplets. In the first couplet, both the lines rhyme, and the same rhyme runs through the whole poem, the rhyme-word being at the end of the second line of each couplet (after the first couplet) as in the *ghazal*. The *qasida* (which means 'purpose') is usually written in praise of someone and is often read in his or her presence, so it is stated that it shouldn't be too long or it might weary the listener. It has a number of sections: i. *matla* - the beginning, ii. *taghazzul* -introduction, iii. *guriz* - the couplets in praise of whoever it is written to, iv. *maqta*- the end. In the *qasida*, the *takhallus* or pen-name of the poet usually does not appear, and if it does it is not necessarily near the end or at the end as in the *ghazal*. Any metre may be used except that used for the *ruba'i*.

The Qit'a

The *qit'a* or 'fragment' must consist of at least two couplets and is similar to a *ghazal* or a *qasida* with the second lines of the couplets all having the same rhyme... but in the first couplet the double-rhyme does not usually appear. It can be composed in any metre except for that of the *ruba'i*. It can be a fragment from a *qasida* or a *ghazal*, or it may be complete in itself. Hafiz and others often used this form to write obituaries on people whom he knew as did many other poets.

The Tomb of Khushal Khan Khattak

Ruba'is...

God… a noble form to be born from dust, is bringing,
and heart with knowledge of great worth, is filling…
and teaches tongue to that Holy Name be praising,
then quite suddenly with mother earth is… mingling.

Gold spurs one on to fame and shames one
too…
that it warms tongues to praise or blame is
true.
By its power most difficult works are made easy,
if steel and gold are wed steel stays steel…
through.

The heavens are off course, their song is wrong,
the saint is grieved by this, fool for it does long.
Drinks of the purest wine to mankind is offered,
but in the gift the germs of illness are, so strong.

If one wishing you wrong is cursing and staring...
let them do it more and more, and don't be caring
even if Khushal, a hundred times you is cursing,
or hundreds saying it, with every prayer, saying.

Those, who fighting to keep the peace trying,

are…

are true ones, who the common good seeking

are:

they, save their grief with all their happy laughter…

carrying on as if their honesty they believing

are!

Like in your heart is laughter, or... grief in there is lying,
your face is full of laughter, or, tears your heart is spilling!
Of everything your heart's the centre, all from it turns,
it is like a judge... that has power to stop or to be allowing.

May everyone be listening to what I am saying

are…

all of those who are envious, they never knowing

are.

Rogues can never be redeemed by good companions…

bad men, fall of good men, sometimes devising

are.

Of the fruits of the orchard that people are eating now,
each as taste on tongue as different, are treating now!
The world also has many bitter fruits that are serving
to show worth of what is sweet, this I'm saying now!

Shaikhs… that such a show of reverence making
are;
if they seek payment, someone them misleading
are!
To their Master, such ones as them are truly worthless:
who… only in the hope of future gain, serving
are.

Each one, at one in seeking their own end
>	is…
a true one, one who seeking end for friend
>	is.
Just reward of that one is a good name and peace,
>	who to aching heart's cure trying to attend
>	is.

One is born free, but soon greed is enslaving
that one…
even more than make a slave, it's corrupting
that one.
As greed fills that one's heart that one is drowning,
and shame's mark cuts deep as it's engraving
that one.

Some men in paths of learning try to shine,
others burn to reveal their piety, O so fine:
it is on great acts of love I've set my heart!
My name God praise for the way I incline!

I said this night that one would be spending

with me

that her face like the moon would be shining

with me,

but, that one remembered none of her promises…

and for that night my luck was not staying

with me.

If one cuts up sugarcane it will be giving sugar,
one cuts open the oyster the pearl it will deliver.
Khushal, don't be giving up less than the stone,
for from some stones comes gold in the crusher!

No matter how much the living keep wailing and
weeping,
the resurrection of who have died... will one day be
happening?
It is impossible... so all those who mourn have to keep on
patiently doing so, until the impossibility they are
realizing!

Gold it is that is working many a miracle!
It makes the shy bold, the dead of life full!
It makes slave a master, maid a mistress:
cold hard steel it can make soft... if it will.

Holiness, there are many who are claiming this...
if words were actions they'd be in heavenly bliss!
God forbid, for if God should their actions note,
Satan would be confessing all cleverness of his!

When the falcon flies low to the sparrow take,
it acts like a hawk and its name does forsake:
the greatest of men are never narrow or mean,
in acts they reveal their greatness, never fake!

Ghazals…

Ah… what a wonderfully delicious wine is this,
that the winebringer, we welcome… bringing is!
Laughter of the bud in the garden is impossible,
if breeze each morning over it makes no passes.
Its advice was this, in regards to nightingale…
morning rip rosebud's garment, from its leaves.
O rose, appreciate the value of the nightingale,
though you bloom in your beauty now, like this.
As the lover's cure depends on heart's objective,
any knowledge of love's disease by physician is?
Except for the beaming face of the beloved don't
imagine that Khushal content with any other is.

Minstrel's *rebeck* again spreads magic in the air
its story it tells and each time it's new to the ear.
Let shaikh prefer cell, I'll keep to my rose-garden:
for my guide all I need are spring flowers so fair!
Problems unending beggars have in filling bellies,
kings worry about governing... of who to beware!
I'd be blessed more if that one always loved me...
but I count as a favour if she drives me to despair.
I'm made happy and sad by the way I'm treated...
to her I say thanks or complain, "O how unfair!"
What else can my destiny be if it isn't this state?
She complains more than my competitor! Beware!
Wineseller in this city is openly plying his trade...
it's obvious the censor favours drinkers, I declare!
If it's counted as sin to love and look at fair faces,
then Khushal Khattak all of his life was a sinner!

I'm acquainted with Aurangzeb's justice and impartiality:
his self-denial and fasts, in matters of faith his orthodoxy;
his own brothers, time after time, cruelly put to the sword;
father beaten in battle, thrown into prison, never to be free!
Even if a person hits head on the ground a thousand times,
or by his fasting bring his spine and navel together to see;
until, coupled with that desire of acting with goodness…
his adorations, devotions, are impositions, lies, obviously.
The way of whose tongue is one and path of heart another,
may his vital organs be mangled, by the knife lacerated be!
Externally the serpent is handsome, symmetrically formed;
but, internally it is not clean, with venom filled, massively.
The acts of men will be many, and their words will be few,
but the acts of the false are few and their boasts are many.
Since Khushal's arm cannot reach to the tyrant from here,
at doom's day may the Almighty upon him, have no mercy!

Why is Aurangzeb, his throne and crown enriching?
For both death will attack, and leave them rotting!
Behind in this world, only his evil name will remain;
knowing whether as Kisra or Hujuj* he was acting!"
Overwhelmed by grief I don't know festival or feast,
although all Delhi's population are happily partying.
All water came into the eyes and heart's fire blazed:
O, can anyone in such a state of mind keep existing?
When a finger is laid on my pulse they all turn pale...
in which way can those doctors my illness be curing?
Separation is cutting up my heart, in the same way as
the falcon, the partridge and quail... goes on tearing!
When two friends are separated by a distant land...
God, of a mere salutation makes them be so longing!
My tears are made through the emotions of the heart
like fire drains out the moisture from meat, roasting.
Ah no, every arrow discharged from fatality's bow...
destiny, a target... poor heart of Khushal, is making!

*Note: *Kisra, or Cyrus, King of Persia, is the model of a just king; and Hujuj bin Yusuf, Governor of Khurasan, under the Khalafah, Abd-ul-Malik, the conception of a perfect tyrant.*

What have men's high and holy days to do with me?
I'm Majnun* in love's wilderness, them I don't see!
That holy day for me, that one I will be celebrating,
is when God reveals beloved Layla's face... clearly.
The real lover wouldn't deny love than deny living:
in the same way sinners in their hearts on sin rely.
That one isn't worth friendship and it is his fault,
who as friend hasn't good faith or any constancy.
So many people are boasting of being a real friend:
among them I've not found truthfulness with me!
From love's hidden, burning, flames God save us:
from grass or wood may is never burn you, totally.
There's no part for thought or meditation in love:
in sight or sound it's made clear to us, eventually.
Each stone doesn't spark when struck with steel:
only the flint can with the tinder work, properly!
Khushal, where else can one find such thoughts
creating rosegarden from your words, beautifully.

*Note: Majnun (about 721 A.D.) which means 'madman' whose real name was Qays, was the famous lover of Layla who came from another tribe in Arabia. Majnun fell in love with Layla when they were children at school together. Unable to contain his love, one day he expressed it and Layla's father, enraged by the scandal of this 'madman' in love with his daughter, refused to allow them to see etch other. Majnun's father, who was the leader of his tribe, tried to reconcile them but to no avail. Layla also loved Majnun. Majnun wandered the hills living with wild animals and composing songs in praise of Layla. Finally their human love became so great that it was transformed into Divine Love by a Perfect Master. Layla became so undernourished from missing him that she finally starved to death. Majnun threw himself on her grave and died there. Their souls mingled with their dust. Many stories and poems have been written about them, the most popular being that by Nizami. See my translation of Nizami's 'Majnun & Layla and my translation of Majnun's own poems: 'Poems of Majnun,' both New Humanity Books, Campbells Creek, 2012.

You were saying, "Stop grieving, for I'm yours and you are mine:"
whether you spoke truly or not, life you've given to mine in decline.
What a lovely disaster you are, but also an incomparable charmer!
If only there wasn't a defect, you've a cruel heart: that, I'd <u>underline!</u>
If the whole of the universe in every direction is filled with beauty…
it would be astonishing if one more beautiful than you did shine.
You've slain so many victims and yet show no pity or any regret…
it matters, when you to shed blood a hundred times, do incline?
As out of your garden or your rosebed I beg for a rose from you…
should you only give a straw to me; I, like rose, to take do resign.
For as long as I exist, it is true that I stay captured by your curls…

in every hair, hundred of hearts will be held captive, like mine!
Whether old or young, all have been distracted because of you…
there's not a person in this town who doesn't find you their valentine.
Look at the cypress, and very quickly one stops looking at it,
when you with your form through the garden walk; tall, so fine!
The prospect of Paradise to come, is bliss to ascetic and clergy;
but Khushal as Paradise here, right now, on meeting you… mine!

When towards his father, a son acts in a perfidious way...
in what way will he show sincerity to others, please say!
See what more deceit must lay inside of that one's heart,
when the hypocrite acknowledges his misdeeds... one day.
I will never pardon the enormous sins of the degenerate...
neither will God forgive sins of fallen angel who must pay.
All of these small hills are like nothing: I'm one who wants
my God to place between us *Kaf* itself, to keep him away!
The conduct of son is known to father better than others...
why do people commend that degenerate to me, anyway?
There is not one liar who can utter falsehood like that one,
there is none who can equal that one in deceit, on any day!
There are thousands of varieties of vanity in that heart...
thousands of boasts of morality, that tongue does display.
That I cherished and brought up such a son, so unfaithful,
was... all for this: that one would go against me, one day!
Really, never let me cast eyes upon him as long as I live...
after death don't let that one near my grave, this... I pray.
Sorrow and grief will, while alive, leave this one's heart...
if fate, to Khushal will grant justice due to come his way!

Note: Kaf... the mythical mountain, the boundary of the world, and surrounding the horizon on all sides.

They are your dark curls waving...
darling, so beautiful and happy...
and eyes, black narcissi, glancing:
darling, so beautiful and happy!
When you gave a kiss, I was intoxicated beyond recognition:
like red wine your lips are tasting;
darling, so beautiful and happy!
Now, that I've with my eyes gazed on this, your lovely cheek,
I know that it's the tulip glowing,
darling; so beautiful and happy!
They who murmur, complaining to others of your tyranny, are
faithless, unreliable and nothing,
darling... so beautiful and happy!
How can that one sleep free from grief or be full of tranquility,
who from you, you're separating
darling, so beautiful, and happy?
Only that one receives your kisses to whom your love's given...
though many you are enrapturing,
darling; so beautiful and happy!
You shower injustice on me, then say: "I have not done this..."
whose did it if you're not it doing,
darling, so beautiful and happy?

You say to Khushal, "Others are more beautiful than me!"
Has there be one more charming,
darling, so beautiful and happy?

Through great sorrow at the Afghans mean-spiritedness,
I have abandoned greatness… into hand taken meanness.
It would be good if even this, in this matter was gained…
I had brought down on the coward my revenge in fullness.
From that time when the jewel of my honour was broken,
I have not left even for a moment free from tears my eyes.
After all my trouble that pearl never came into my hands,
so I did draw up my boat on the sea's shore, nevertheless.
This waist of mine, that in resistance was a mountain…
from worry, disappointment, to Mughal I bent, I confess.
But, allow good fortune once again begin to be helping me
so it can relieve me from the weight of this load… no less!
This misery should never be compared to any other grief,
though I've had a thousand other woes, not of such stress.
The back of fortune and the world's are turned upon me…
from grief I turned face from all to Mughal, this I express.
If it was in my power, or if it was still my own free-will…
I would never even two paces, to them walk under duress.
  I've to listen to crooked words from the mouths of those
to whom during my life I did never a straight one express.
Outcries of my own people and even strangers, affect me;
although I'd screen myself from any whisper's foul caress.

I am now so ashamed of those proud and boastful words,
that before every one would from my lips, myself express!
A hundred criticisms and indignities are heaped upon me,
who guarded himself from reproaches… and scornfulness.
It is for this reason that the elephant throws dust on head:
I acquainted that elephant, with Khushal's sorrowfulness!

Everywhere, there is lamination,
due to the hand of death;
in each place and habitation,
due to the hand… of death!
The human form God created for the sake if death itself:
in this world… evil and vexation,
due to the hand of death!
All of the prophets and the saints that have ever existed,
all into earth have been hidden…
due to the hand of death!
Without an ounce of doubt, in the end all these fair abodes
will come to ruin and desolation,
due to the hand of death!
Come, and be occupied with provisions for your journey;
for despatched is every caravan…
due to the hand of death!
Khushal, even if your body should be that of a Shah Jahan,
you'd sadly depart, even then…
due to the hand of death!*

*Note: Referring to the unhappy end of the emperor Shah Jahan, dethroned and imprisoned by Aurangzeb, his son.

One time, I was always wise… and wiser
even now, I am!
I was always mad, beside myself: madder,
even now, I am!
Nearness is, not farness: from God, separation is unreal…
I was dwelling with God, and a dweller,
even now… I am!
Since I entered into the world, I've come to know myself…
I was a treasury of mysteries… a treasure,
even now, I am!
Mention of my worth in the world, is made far and near…
among folks I was a character; a character,
even now, I am!
When veil from God's face was withdrawn, I saw a Light;
immediately I was a moth; a moth I swear,
even now I am!
Arrows of that One's eyelashes are my life's misfortune:
for an age I was a target… target, I declare
even now I am!
When He made me a friend, He turned me from any other:
stranger to the world I became, a stranger
even now, I am!

That Ocean all-surrounding, boundless and unfathomable,

of Ocean I was a pearl; its pearl I share,

"Even now I am!"

In the same way, with Beloved, without any go-between…

as I, Khushal, used to be in love, the lover,

even now, I am!

Just like the wind, every moment, life is passing away;
and so, let every man be remembering death every day!
Since the foundation of each one's life is based on air,
what reliance can be placed on this life... please, say!
The dust of man is leavened with mortality's water;
Omnipotent's hand kneads it in forty days, from clay!
The saints and the prophets have gone into the tomb...
honestly, you'd that they had never existed at all, say!
If you'd consider it closely, time of life here is nothing:
no one in it attained his desires and hopes, in any way.
If you really seek Eternal Life, then I say to you this...
war with infidels of lusts of the flesh, don't go astray.
The careful traveller whose journey is lying before him,
takes provision along, according to length of the way!
Come, O Khushal, cut away your heart from all else...
and in the hope of meeting that One, let it in joy, stay!

In the tomb will be no worldly ambitions, no vanities too:
your own good deeds, nothing else, will be going with you!
Understand this… without the parrot, the cage is useless:
soul could be likened to a parrot and body like its cage too!
Be very careful that it may not be lost to you, altogether…
for, like a pearl of great price, is breath you blow and blew.
Whoever throws this precious pearl away without a profit,
that such a one has less brains than a field's beast, is true.
Pass near to the graves of the chiefs and nobles of the land
and see from their dust, thorns and brambles grow through.
Whatever has happened cannot be changed… and so why
then do you show such apprehension… and even dread too?
It's your lot to bear from the world, at most a shroud away:
and that too will be just eight or nine yards, or ten, for you!
All these things, my dear, behind you shall be remaining…
whether pretty girls, noble steeds or robes of fine satin too!
Be ready, O Khushal, because the time of departure's here:
in every direction can be heard sound of warning bell, anew!

The affairs of the world have all upside-down been turned;
those ways are not as I saw them before, they've changed!
To the father the son's displaying the actions of an enemy:
to the mother, daughters act like rival wives, let it be said.
In your house there'll not be two brothers staying together,
who have not a thousand iniquities into their hearts... fed.
The scavenger now feasts on *pilau,* rice and sweetmeats...
to unclean things, Mohammed's descendants, are now led.
Those, who kings honoured and trusted, are now thieves...
and in royal courts highway-robbers are now to be trusted.
The nightingales and parrots fly astonished, in the wilds;
and crows and ravens caw and croak, above the flowerbed!
Steeds from Babylon eke out an existence upon dry grass;
while asses of a tanner gets a stipend, on provisions based.
Fools, exempt from cares and anxieties, sleep peacefully...
as the prudent and wise have misfortunes, by the hundred.
The meanest slave is assuming authority over his master;
slave-girls than mistress of the house, are more honoured.
Ah no, O Khushal, in the days of the emperor Aurangzeb,
all house-born servants are a lot, contemptible, wretched!*

**Note: This is a ghazal influenced by a famous ghazal by Hafiz... see my translation of the Divan of Hafiz, New Humanity Books, 1986, 2012 (ghazal number 442).*

If Your heart had a little compassion, how wonderful
it would be!
If a little of Your love was given to me... how merciful
it would be!
Through grief for You, I am weeping, lamenting at Your
threshold:
if Your ear was inclined to my complaining, how rightful
it would be!
Whoever are blaming and crying out against me for my
loving You,
if they knew of Your beauty's perfection, how beautiful
it would be!
Those now boasting before the world of their austerity and
self-control,
if they refrained from looking at You... how respectful
it would be!
After my death, if my grave should happen to be situated
in a place
where path of beautiful You, always is... how delightful
it would be!
In the alleyway there are many greyhounds and other dogs
lying about:

if I was lucky to be counted among them… how fateful it would be!

My grief for You is impossible to be quenched in one short existence;

if the life of Khushal was very, very long… how plentiful it would be!

Don't say to me, "Why do you say: 'by You,
I swear!'"
If I don't swear by You, by whom but You, do
I swear?
Honestly, You are the very light of these eyes of mine;
by those black eyes of Yours… this is so true,
I swear!
The day is Your countenance and Your curls the night:
I swear by the morning and by the night too…
I swear!
I swear You are my very life and my soul in this world,
and besides that, nothing else: my life to You,
I swear!
It is true, that You are the idea engrossing my mind…
every hour, every moment: by my God, too…
I swear!
Dust of Your feet's an ointment for these eyes of mine:
by dust beneath my feet, through and through
I swear!
My heart always desires to be with You, desperately…
by this ardent longing of mine… again to You
I swear!

When You're laughing they are nothing in comparison:
all the rubies and pearls. By Your laughter too
I swear!
It is true, I am only Your lover and I am Yours only…
this, I, Khushal, by Your lovely face, as adieu,
I swear!

It is false that any evil or any misfortune from the stars is coming…
all good and evil, suffering and worry, from God's decree is emanating.
If their excellence is in their colour then what about their fragrance?
For flowers made of paper are like similar to flowers when looking!
Fortune could be likened to a child, in its disposition and ways…
because when the child gives one any thing, soon it… it is regretting.
When prosperity of the world turns its face away from the ignorant…
those wise, their words and their actions that follow, find amazing.
And when the wise may not be in possession of any of its wealth…
in the world's eyes that one is a blockhead or a fool for not complaining.
When I had much power and influence my words were like pearls…

but now I am satisfied, if even like corals, others they are appreciating.

Let us be seeing what happenings after this, will reveal to us...

even though in the meantime, the world will simply go on chattering.

As much as love of wealth brings success, it brings much misery...

for all those who gather much of it, miserable they are all becoming.

I am really the same Khushal, but now they do not value me...

because it's about the Afghans, that I keep doing all of my complaining.

O so many people that I have remembered,
have come and passed away, like the wind.
Truly, they arrive and depart in such a way,
they seem to have no place to stay… I find.
This, is an astonishing and vast workshop
the Great Master set up… for humankind.
Cast your eyes on the bubble in the stream:
what is it and its base… its origin, to find?
You're that too, if you can only understand:
to you a good example is given… to unwind.
Concerning yourself, you know… nothing:
you know nothing, you are no mastermind!
What is the meaning of all grief and misery,
and why did you happiness again then find?
O Khushal, since it is all so very, very hard,
is this your heart, or a lump of steel, unkind?

Upon the difficult path of love, there is peril everywhere:
every footstep that I take on it, I place my life in danger.
Tear my chest apart… see how my heart is full of blood,
it's only from grief for You that my heart's now bloodier.
The gentle rain of Your kindness does not fall upon me,
so Your love's seed planted in my heart may be a grower!
Your treasured secret, even to my tongue I'll not impart;
a secret reaching the tongue, is a tale told over and over.
With regard to love I'm ignorant as to what a thing it is:
but, its effect is coming from beauty; this, is what I hear.
Who's that one having attained that love beyond words?
Although, every one boasts about success in this matter!
It was when you and I were not yet, that love was born…
it cannot be said that you or me have been love's creator!
O Khushal… hide from the world all of the woes of love!
But, how can I conceal that, which it of it, is the knower?

The faithlessness of the world has become obvious to me;
so, I drew my pen through the word 'friendship'... heavily.
Like when fire reaches to brushwood and will soon go out;
same with pangs of absence, they last for a few days only.
Than sun's light, that of true knowledge is even brighter...
don't let anyone leave radiance such as this for an eternity!
Witness what a form so admirable comes out of each drop!
It's true the works of the Almighty of Himself are worthy!
You O nightingale, would have once given rose your heart,
if market of its beauty were it keep flourishing, continually.
From now on there will not be peace like this for me again,
since I've become aware, O solitude, of your value to me!
All who through their effort try to gain world's prosperity,
intelligence of such people in my sight is less than... a pea.
From whom shall I be seeking to obtain a panacea as this:
prepared for one purpose... to be for my pains, the remedy?
Since the calamity of separation is always linked with it...
why is the beauty of any beloved praised indiscriminately?
As the gem has become less valued than a mere kauri shell,
there is no jeweller with sight to distinguish them properly.
Seeing that wherever may be beauty, the heart is there...
to what degree shall Khushal's self-denial, a praising be?

By the laughter of the happy and joyful…

I swear:

and by the lamentations of the sorrowful,

I swear!

By the inebriation of those intoxicated with wine;

by the monk's piety, abstinence… dutiful,

I swear!

By the hundred happenings, meetings, friendships,

and the thousands of partings… so pitiful,

I swear!

By the beautiful and fragrant roses of the spring…

by the nightingales melodies, beautiful…

I swear!

Compared to which, graceful cypress is as naught,

by that tall stature and form symmetrical,

I swear!

They, are tinged with the antimony of expression:

by those narcissus eyes, so dark, powerful,

I swear!

That… which is even more slender than even a hair,

by that slight waist of Yours, so fanciful…

I swear!

On account of which, lovers pine away and die…
by that beauty, by that which is graceful…
I swear!
By that which comes from direction of the Beloved,
and breath of morning breeze, delightful…
I swear!
By who is the bearer of the message for a meeting…
by footsteps of bringer of news, wonderful,
I swear!
In that which there's not the least bit of insincerity,
and by all the truthfulness of the truthful…
I swear!
With each of all these many oaths and declarations,
a hundred thousand times I state… in full,
I swear
that I love You so much more than even life itself…
and this, myself, a Khattak called Khushal,
I swear!

Every moment that a person, work may be seeking,
better off I believe is one made to work, for nothing.
If those who are sick don't work, they are excused;
but, why should not the healthy man earn a living?
And even if you do not have any work of your own;
I say to you don't sit still, useless, and not working.
Every amusement that may stop worries, is good…
whether chess, backgammon or pleasure of chasing.
Every hour and moment a man's state is different…
only the Creator of the world stays never changing.
Your name… O Khushal, will be remembered in the
world, for truly a great work, is what you are doing!

Winebringer, I request that from the special flagon
a few cups of that finest wine to me be passing on.
For such a spring to go without wine to drink to it
is such a sin, that cannot be condoned by anyone.
I must repent of wine my religious guide tells me,
but I am sure such repentance in spring is wrong!
Spring won't last so let us go on an evening walk
until the dawn, through this paradise of a garden.
The wild narcissi are spread out like a troop ahead
in a brave, a fine parade telling spring to come on!
Dawn breeze, buds of every colour you've in field
set free and so Khushal greets all, "Open, open!"

I am in love with those eyes of yours... look at me!
I'm a Hindu slave of your curls, me don't set free!
With the figure and the charms that you possess
it would be wonderful, if like you, another did be.
To you there is no equal in loveliness and grace...
that you're cruel and without pity is a great pity.
You turn from me although I die of grief for you,
why has love in your heart become dark for me?
I'll never leave your door nor the place you stay,
even if without any fire you consume me, cruelly.
If you do a thousand cruelties to me do not think
the love of my heart towards you changed will be.
I'm happy, sunk in contempt in dust of your door;
but nowhere else, even if on a throne sitting is me!

Wine's intoxication comes soon, is soon disappearing;
but... eternal intoxication, a drunkard is never leaving.
Although in this world I am notorious for debauchery
I will still never give away the ways of wine-drinking!
Even if the ruler throws me into prison I'll not grieve,
for the liberty of the free is from time's very beginning.
I find friendship, relationship, doesn't exist: all is fake
since the ways and usages of mankind I was knowing.
Though now sorrowful, I'm happy in hope joy comes...
for after the night has passed the day is soon coming!
In the depth of the ocean the pearl of our longing lies;
after it, into its dark abyss the diver keeps on diving!
That fish that may sense danger from the sharp hook
won't, due to caution, from depth to shore be looking.
Thoughts of lover's heart are like the deepest ocean...
at times it billows in fury, at times is calmly sleeping.
From heart of Khushal love for the beloved never goes:
it's like the love of idolater for idol one is worshipping.

Such a great amount of misery is today in my family
that at the sight of our troubles the world is uneasy!
In path of own father a degenerate son sows thorns;
but the good son's a rose-garden blooming eternally.
Hell on earth the incapable, worthless son's making.
but a worthy son is a paradise in his father's family.
In house of parents a good child is a lamp shining…
a graceless, bad one is in that home the dark, murky.
Mature his nature is of a trap and an animal of prey;
good conduct of a child is better, even if young is he.
A vicious son destroys name of father, grandfather…
even if a banner of their greatness is held up, highly!
The good son struggles for good name and reputation,
while the good-for-nothing regards more so, the belly.
Truly, since dogs that are described were born to him,
I begin to doubt if Khushal, a human being could be!

To that old man who sighs after his youthfulness, say...
"What is this old man, you laugh at your beard today?"
Since in a year the wild rue will have youth and old age
than the fate of us humans that of it is far better I say.
At times a man becomes so full at a table he can't eat,
other times he rolls eyes on it, his greed he does betray.
In their wishes, words and in the way they are acting
the people of the world doubt each other in every way.
Now that my beard is white why should I fear death,
when friends with black beards... have passed away?
Anyone under whose sway the whole earth once was
look closely and you'll see all under the earth, today!
The people of the world are like shifting bits of sand,
for truly they roll over and upset each other each day.
With my eyes I have seen the dreaded furnace of fate:
Khushal like dried-up grass it consumes in every way.

Beloved, there will not be another so loving as me:
another in such despair for you, you will never see.
You killed me, then over me you were mourning...
what a beloved, what a love; my death and elegy!
Your lovely face is a garden, flowers of all hues...
enjoy spring for a garden like this won't again be!
Look at the tulip, a heart-burnt flower all covered:
no martyr such a winding sheet wore... so bloody!
Look at that sable-like hair on your lovely cheeks:
no such spikenards in world's garden found a lily.
If one made a cover from petals, they'd irritate...
for, no one else but you has such a delicate body.
You, who I look at day and night inside myself...
poor Majnun during his whole life did never see!
The female Hindu's right by custom or by law is
to sit on her lover's pyre to burn away faithfully.
Some, out of sorrow, wring hands, weep for you:
it isn't death but life if like this dying one can be.
I enjoyed the bliss of Iram in your court, inside...
such a home is Khushal's, with fate he is happy!
You'll know such lines in Persian won't be heard
like those Khushal in Pashtu recites so perfectly.

God makes me such a form be adoring,
if it's wrong, it's as it is;
and if before that idol I'm worshipping
if it's wrong, it's as it is!
All say, "You're in love;" I deny on oath, say, "I am?"
In such a way to everyone I am lying:
if it's wrong, it's as it is!
Others can lead any lives they want, I don't criticize:
I travel the world my eyes feasting…
if it's wrong, it's as it is!
If when I'm leaving this life your name leaves my lips
they'll me as infidel be condemning:
if it's wrong, it's as it is!
If I should be offered Paradise or a way to your street,
for eternity your street I am having:
if it's wrong, it's as it is.
The only way I can praise you is to praise you in poetry.
I say it all over for all to be hearing:
if it's wrong, it's as it is.
When young I aged quickly by always telling the truth,
of the world an enemy I was making:
if it's wrong, it's as it is!

All shaikhs, priests, the pious talk slyly behind back:
to world's face I say all I'm meaning…
if it's wrong, it's as it is!
If red wine inspires others, Khushal just looks inside
the winehouse to see them all drinking:
if it's wrong, it's as it is!

With my fate I'm content, for like a snake again
I've in one piece let go my grief's old, dead skin.
Again I can see beauty and grace with my eyes
although for awhile fate dulled them... within.
Mist and clouds, dust and smoke have all gone
from sun's bright eye that now on ice can shine.
Of patience or spirit may God never deprive us
when in this world a tragedy does again begin!
In each market-place time had me wandering...
it taught me all to know of worth of each thing.
Growth again comes in spring to enliven tree...
although autumn sees each leaf that has fallen.
The fate of Khushal's better than Shah Jahan's:
although a captive, the Lord restored me again.

I'm a winehouse frequenter, so don't expect
propriety...
All night until dawn and all day until the sun sets,
one full glass after another I am drinking...
continually.
Your fair face, who exists to compare it to the sun?
Sun can be likened to a lamp... dawn, your
beauty!
O pious, don't cover eyes so fair face can't be seen:
it is now declared a lawful act to that face
see!
Winebringer, when bad luck strikes pour more wine,
as it fills up... it shines than a lamp more
brightly!
Censor, Khushal's here, prepare to meet in the field:
cover yourself in wine, 'that armour of the
devotee!'

Like the wind each moment one's life is passing,
each one should of his death be always thinking.
As the foundation of one's life is set only in air,
upon such a life as this can one ever be relying?
To wet Adam's clay grief's waters were used...
when for forty dawns God it kept on kneading.
Saints and prophets all departed into the grave:
one could say the world no foundation is having.
If you think hard on it life's nothing here, below:
here, no one ever received what he was desiring.
If you are seeking eternal life, this I'll tell you...
against lusts of your flesh eternally be waging!
That wayfarer whose journey is still up ahead,
what ever is needed will be provisions taking.
Khushal set heart on this, take it from all else,
so in hope of seeing God it can go on rejoicing.

At midnight while I slept beloved came to my bed:
a beautiful, radiant face, breast... jasmine-scented!
She wore a dress of many colours, laced with gold,
she looked from head to toe, shining, transfigured!
Her face was as fair as the soul of a true-believer,
black as a infidel's were curls spilling off her head!
No shawl covered head, in hand a glass of wine...
she seemed beside herself and by the wine excited.
From anklets tinkling and brows amulets clinking
I woke up, and as one does away I abruptly shied.
I wondered if it was a *houri* or *peri* of Paradise...
that came in dead of night to make me fascinated.
Like archer's bow brow bent, lashes like arrows,
teeth expensive pearls guarding lips so sugared!
With that laughing voice she said taunting me:
"Blind one look at me... why should I be feared?
Don't you recognize me, I'm that one you love:
none can be known more beautiful, let it be said.
In town are many who are desiring my mouth...
you're fortunate, to the rest you I've preferred!"
Kisses beyond counting she pressed to my lips:
as though from her a cup of red wine I drained.

We shared my bed all night and our love's secret:
yet, still the joy of being with her… never ended.
Finally the voice of a *muezzin* called all to pray…
at dawn she left me… to the end, she still flirted.
When one loved, must leave one, full of sorrow…
that a new dawn comes for lover is then wasted.
When Khushal is grieving for one loved like her,
such pain is from fire, his bed seems surrounded.

Why won't you go down the street where Friend's living?
You beg door to door, but not where One, you is calling!
From begging door to door let ashes be on your head...
this lesson I tell you learn, O you wretched one, begging!
Than lovely flowers of spring you are more beautiful: why turn from Friend's face to at spring roses be looking?
Your Friend's at hand, no matter what you desire... yet both your eyes are blind, of yourself knowing nothing!
I'm always telling you this, I only wish good for you: think about provisions as a journey you'll soon be making.
On every side are chikors, partridges; black, white... you have a hawk with you though its wings you're clipping!
You've seed, fallow field, plough-team that's ready: everything is available, yet you won't begin your ploughing!

One day's a reckoning, each hair weighed, counted:
in your account-book come and what is there be
seeing.
Listen before it is too late, enemies are everywhere:
Khushal, know that this road is dangerous to be
travelling!

You said: "Do not grieve no more for me to be yours, or you mine."

I was brought back to life by this you said honestly... or by design.

You're bewitching in beauty, your loveliness without equal: If only you didn't have a fault, a cruel witch's heart, a bad sign!

If the whole world had only people with forms all beautiful, it would be a great miracle... one as beautiful as you, so superfine!

Although many are killed by love for you, you do not care: does a chieftain care if he commits bloody acts, not one sign!

When from your rosegarden's scented beds I ask for a rose, if you gave me but one twig for a rose I would take it as mine.

As long as breath in me stays I stay a slave to those curls, from each hair that thrilled a hundred hearts, hanging to combine!

Whether old men or beardless youths all cry for you, lost! In all the town is not one man who to love you, doesn't whine?

Look at the tall cypress how when you appear it's ignored:
when you stroll about the field all rooted trees wilt into decline!
They say a future Paradise exists where priest or pious go:
Khushal's on earth today, seeing you says, "Paradise, is mine!"

Spring is here and again in the fields narcissi are
everywhere…
I can see breeze blow hyacinths wildly like some
hair!
For just five days rose grown by garden is fair and fresh;
on the sixth it is wilting away like it was never
there.
Before rose the nightingale mad with love is prostrating,
like Brahmin lays head to worship idol, back in
India.
The cypress should be for one a true symbol of humility:
look at how despite its height it has a modest
air.
Until now Khushal any other kind of wine hasn't drunk:
this in him is from when First Day's cup he did
share!*

*Note: This couplet refers to the Covenant that God made on the First Day i.e. before the Creation, in God's Imagination. God created (in His Infinite Imagination) all the souls that were possible to create, and He asked them: "Am I NOT your God?" This of course was something of a trick question, and not without a sense of humour. Some, out of love, not wishing to be rude by not answering answered: "Yes!" (In other words: You are NOT our God). These were the lovers of God. Others did not answer. God then manifested all of the souls into creation, some of them being lovers (here Khushal claims to have remembered saying "yes" and so was one of these), and others, those who had to learn from the lovers to try to love and to say "yes" to God, even though to try is the best that one can do.

The word in Persian for 'yes' has a number of meanings: it also means 'mistake' or 'calamity' or 'curse.' Hafiz claims to have drunk the cup of love for God from before the Creation was formed, and so his drunkenness is of seeing God in the whole of His creation.

From ignorance what disasters are caused by the
inexperienced...
not even knowing ABC's, by himself a priest is
called!
Country bumpkin who has never left farm for open plain,
will talk easily about the plain of Kerbala, as if
recalled!*
And, faith's sword originally made to strike the infidel...
an idolater puts on to good Muslims soon make
dead.
Each wise man must think his wisdom is a like a curse...
when he is so often by a hundred worries being
afflicted.
If someone thieves or uses trickery, does bloody actions,
or is fornicating... by these an evil character is
revealed,
but of all of the evil natures this world can be revealing
one is worse a thousand times... to lie, let it be
said!
When that artist Mars reveals how he can compose...
it is the time for Mercury to put down his pen,
disenchanted!*

These couplets Khushal writes are not made to hear...
they are composed for enjoyment, for him to be
entertained.

*Notes: The plain at Kerbala in Iraq was where the grandson
of Prophet Mohammed, Husain, was martyred.
*The planet Mercury is known as 'Heaven's clerk'.
In this couplet Khushal is saying he is Mars.

Young, fiery winebringer, in glass tinted azure-blue…
give a goblet full of the wine that each ill will sees to.
One glass of wine all the world's tributes isn't worth;
so censor, leave me wine, though I am a ruin to view.
If with crown you want royalty beg near winehouse:
wine-drinking's popularity comes from drinking too!
From monastery to a cell is not a road with a profit,
better to take winebringer's cup, in it is joy for you!
Winebringer, sun-like face, moon-browed, don't go:
for Khushal a crystal goblet brimming over will do!

Under your raven curls, not a plain cheek is hiding...
I see over roses petals of hyacinth, plaited... curling.
I was always seeking you, and finally I am fortunate
to find such a bewitching friend all are of you talking.
One can think of Majnun, Farhad, Wamiq or Azra:
a hundred blessings on all who for love were living.*
All others pass away but if it's any who don't die it
is those we remember in this world that is passing.
Why listen to other stories in theirs is all to know:
remember the candle; while you weep be laughing.
No matter what region Khushal happens to be in,
look and see your tips of curls my heart entwining.

*Note: All famous lovers in Persian poetry and history.

One who is mad, how would you treat such a one?
The madman can only be in chains or in a prison!
My heart is stolen by that one, chained by curls:
like a fish to see, by angler's hook trapped upon!
In this world there is no joy but that one to see,
compared to it royal throne's pleasures are none.
Lucky one in Canaan who took Joseph from pit,
received bliss as under a lucky star he was born.
In the sweet-seller's shop is a tiny Hindu child,
or maybe it is a dark mole that your lip is upon?
In spring wander around Seray's fine country…
not in Kabul's outskirts, or Kashmir of renown!
Ah, Khushal, with waters of Landdal compare
the streams of milk of Paradise, that gush on!

If, through love like Mansur did you are an 'infidel',
only then to God's one law you'll conform as well.*
Meaning nothing will be serious talk of the wise…
when with all those who're mad for love you dwell.
To you, bitter will be all the world tastes as sweet:
after tasting real love of Friend, all else will repel.
True peace will come and fill your heart when you
leave company of others, find a quiet, private cell.
You will find world's enticements laughable when
from contentment's store you buy escape from hell.
Let only once the Alchemist's eye glance upon you
and even if you are only dust you'll be gold as well.
A pearl without the right lustre is without value…
worth is not the form, but what inside does dwell.
Khushal, the idol-temples are now old and ruined;
like Abraham cry at them, of your inner self tell!*

*Notes: The famous and infamous Perfect Master and martyr Mansur Hallaj (d.919 A.D.), who was sentenced to death for saying: "I am the Truth (Anal Haq)." Much has been written about Hallaj and his famous (and infamous) statement. If the reader wishes to follow up his life and writings, a list is given below. To me, the meaning of this couplet in its context is that it was Hallaj's Karma or Fate to make that true statement and suffer the consequences; but it does not mean that others who experience the same, God-realisation, have to proclaim it to the whole world, unless they have a particular role to play in this creation by doing so. On Mansur Hallaj's life and sayings see: 'Muslim Saints and Mystics' by Farid ud-Din Attar trans. by A.J. Arberry R.K.P. pp. 264-272; 'The Kashf al-Mahjub: The Oldest Persian Treatise on Sufism' by Hujwiri. trans. by R.A. Nicholson, Luzac, U.K. 'Diwan of al Hallaj' trans. into French by Louis Massignon, Paris 1955 (Documents Spiritual S.10); 'The Passion of Hallaj' by Louis Massignon, Princeton University Press. For his poems see my 'Mansur Hallaj: Selected Poems' New Humanity Books, 2012.

*Abraham overthrew the idols in the temple, going against his tribe in doing so. See Koran xxi, 51.

God has given to me a mind,
that all clear... I always find.
Secrets of earth and heavens
in my heart God has defined.
God's shown me everything
in my heart: I am, not blind!
In others are the black night:
Khushal makes dawn, a find!

This spring is such a glorious thing,
nightingales everywhere they sing:
on Arabian mares some proudly sit,
others hunters they are mounting…
upon their wrists rare hawks perch,
everywhere fine game abounding…
in the lead there is a fine old falcon
younger hawks are him respecting:
upon the leash greyhounds are held
when time comes they'll be running:
from all troubles a heart that's free,
thoughts only of the beloved having:
Khushal, for such happiness as this,
would the whole world be sacrificing.

*Whenever, to any one friend a word I have said,
it's known through the world so fast it's spread.
If you're hopeful that you'll never feel ashamed
before another, keep all in your heart, not said!
If the chikor was never calling out in the valley
would one take a hawk out to make them dead?
When from lush meadows black partridge calls
by hawk or falcon he is soon of plumes stripped.
When my lips let slip not a word no one spoke:
any breath one lets out is a story manipulated!
Secret words I'd said by dawn the village knew
after I'd to my son that night intimately talked.
Reward of many years is many devoted friends,
of those thousands not one in… to be confided!
Khushal, if your heart must bleed let it be inside
and from friend or stranger keep it all concealed.*

Like an arrow is requiring an archer to make it fly,
poetry needs a skill that only in magician does lie.
To weigh words properly heart must be balanced,
that one too many words is uneven, too hard a try!
On an ink-black horse Truth's bride is mounted...
as over face, the veil of metaphor, she does apply.
But, in her eyes that flirtation is still lying there,
in hundreds of winks, winning ways, sighs, a cry.
With jewels of art of forms her dress embroidered,
simile of sandalwood... perfumed with patchouli!
Alliteration and jingles are the anklets of that one,
a necklace of rhyme around crystal throat, in a tie.
In her flirtatious look the elegance of her is seen...
yet from head to foot her form remains a mystery.
The humble crow or wild kite brought into a poem
will fly and hunt for hearts like falcons in the sky.
The wise one's the one who says his say but once:
wise everywhere know, that wit's soul is brevity.
When in his mother tongue Khushal first wrote,
to Pashtu language he a new beauty did supply.

Everywhere you look there is more wailing
　　　　due to death's hand,
in each place is grief and more suffering...
　　　　due to death's hand.
When God made the form of Adam it was to die:
　　　through world destruction is happening
　　　　due to death's hand.
Prophets God sent us, though being from on high,
　　　they all ended up under the earth lying
　　　　due to death's hand.
Listen, best you be prepared for what is up ahead;
　　　the caravan is on its way to an ending
　　　　due to death's hand.
Khushal, though you should be the world's king...
　　　sadly you've to eventually be leaving,
　　　　due to death's hand.

You're no Joseph, no matter how handsome you be…
you are not wiser than Luqman, no matter your clarity.*
If you are the king of the country with many following,
remember in your heart that Solomon was more kingly.
How many sages, kings or handsome heroes existed?
They came and they left and now they're names only!
No one will ever stay, only a name is remembered:
the evil are remembered for that, good for being godly.
If you hear name of Hajjaj you'll hear Nashirwan's:
the infidel justice saved, the Muslim spoiled by brutality.*
While you are still alive is the right time to do good:
to have regrets in the grave gains one nothing… obviously.
That one's an infidel who's a slave to one's own lust:
the real believer is the one who takes his faith… seriously.

That we all will die is a fact that cannot be ignored:
but doubts are about who in grave resting will
be!
One dying certain in faith will be happy at the time:
who in an honoured grave is put, Koran read
reverently.
Now old age is here and the time of youth has gone:
Khushal, put all else away, for the grave get
ready.

*Notes: Joseph was said to have been so beautiful women would go mad on seeing him. Luqman was the wisest man of his time.
*Hajjaj was the Arab governor of Iraq in early Islam and was a bloodthirsty tyrant. Nashirwan was the Zoroastrian king of Persia in the 6th century A.D. who was nicknamed 'the Just'.

If in your heart you'd fear a bit, some hesitation,
it'd be good…
so that a little of your love to me you'd lay upon,
it'd be good!
When from despair and love for you I weep at your door,
if you'd only to my complaints and tears listen,
it'd be good.
As I will not hide I'm in love many try to shut me up…
if only they'd see how beautiful is your form…
it'd be good!
All those boasting of their piety and abstinence today,
if they looked at you, made such a claim, then,
it'd be good.
If after I die my grave happened to be in a happy spot
so that by it each day came by a beautiful one,
it'd be good.
In your street many dogs, hounds, curs are basking…
O if I could only be one of them, lying unseen,
it'd be good!
Short life he might have won't be enough to love you:
if more lives to love you are to Khushal given,
it'd be good!

If it's a king on a throne or dervish in a monastery
there are many upon the path... if only lost like me.
Upon the name of the Almighty I call all the time:
O if only those friends of mine all acted similarly.
O, if only that one was a woman and not a man...
who's acting not like a real man as far as I can see.
I have more sons than are possible to be counted...
if only for some of them I could say, "Brave is he!"
The hills and the valleys are all filled with them...
if only when they fought successful was the army!
It is the darkest night of despair I've experienced:
if only dawn of the day of joy came... eventually!
There is no man who could find harm in Khushal:
O if only that one knew how sunk so low was he.

The true worth of the rose, tell me...
who knows?
It is the nightingale and honey-bee,
who knows!
In the whole world there are only a few knowing
the skills of alchemy... how many,
who knows?
About you, all of the world may not know much,
but you know you and you know me
who knows.
Your body is lovely but your inner nature is not:
I am Khushal, I am the one, truly...
who knows.

Much better than all of an empire.... I say
is to be having a healthy body in each way.
Though to be wealthy in the world is good,
having honour is worth more upon any day.
If one has purity, and one is also sincere...
it is better than respect, coming one's way.
Contentment, it is something so powerful
it can free a person from grief, right away.
To be prudent in everything that you do...
has so many advantages, too many to say!
Is it possible to call that which is given to
another as a favour, generosity? No way!
The worst kind of hell the earth has to offer
is to have to be with a fool, an hour, a day!
Khushal, make sure intentions stay good:
that intended to be good should good stay.

When against my will I'm kept away from you
    day and night…
I can't rest and I can't sleep and I can't eat too
    day and night.
My heart only remembers beloved's face and dark curls…
    each hour that passes and my heart gets through
    day and night.
I sing praises of that one's face and I praise that long hair:
    with pen's tip, by word of mouth, dusk, dawn too,
    day and night!
I would sacrifice forever sweet-scented musk and camphor,
    if a message would come to me from where are you
    day and night.
Khushal, would give the finest rose-scented jams as alms
    if you would even abuse me, no matter what you do
    day and night.

When one, one's own weaknesses is seeing...
one who can be called wise only then is being.
And the ignorance of one can't be covered up
by oneself again and again... again praising!
One, who has a close relationship with God,
about any calamities will never be worrying.
And that one who knows 'you will not find',*
in the world faith's demands will be fulfilling.
One will be receiving the trust of all others...
if one's words honesty are always revealing.
And when one the store of contentment has,
to not one other that one is then beholding.
That one will make life eternal a homeland
who makes passing like Khushal's passing.

*Note: Koran iii, 86.

Winebringer, serve wine again, it's the day of spring's festivity...
once again the time has come when party-goers drink freely.
All of the sky is bright with the sun that seems everywhere, so dazzling is its magnificence, it blinds us with its beauty!
Everywhere that I'm looking and in all that face I'm seeing ever since it was seen so much, now it nowhere can I see!
That one is one that we can say, has found the life eternal... the one who by that intoxicated glance is martyred, fortunately.
These times make all suffer the same with so many ordeals like Joseph when into court at Egypt was sold into slavery.
Even though my beloved has left me to go to a far off place, in my heart to see all marks and signs of that one is easy.
Those who with the dogs around that one's door are found beyond all others are not only fortunate but they're lucky!

To make one more beautiful makeup's art is often needed,
but for the one whose beauty is real it is not ever
necessary!
When the name of poor Khushal that one let from lips fall,
this day of all of his life was made into one of real
festivity!

Even if it's the wise or fools, the honest or thieves too,
I don't recognise even one to take my path and be true.
To stand beside me in this time of need I see no friend:
by their many empty words they console me? Untrue!
People struggle through crowds, to try to get to me…
like many a determined ant are they, grain to get to!
But when to motivate them the grain runs out again,
to such a barren end they'll never try to get through.
Khushal, don't give up mountain goat you wounded:
it is a track its blood marks clearly enough… for you.

A man is what his motive him is making…
like clothes upon one's form are depending.
An elephant can be thrown by a rhinoceros:
what is an ant and the strength it's having?
It was not all donkeys taking Jesus' weight:
it isn't all heads that riches can be carrying.
Don't go and be looking at another's face…
the worth of one is in the acts one is doing!
I'll tell you this: I'm any person's slave who
is good to look at and worthwhile is acting.
If the character and looks of one pleases one
a greater gift than this one can't be having.
Open your ears to the sayings of Khushul:
in his words are joy, and some flavouring!

Though one tries a thousand times with many a skilful way...
one cannot make one's eternal fate change even for one day.
Like an elephant is the strength of destiny that is eternal:
compared to it, anyone's thoughts are like insects... I say.
Alexander the Great looked for the Water of Eternal Life
but it was Khizer who found it and the other lost his way.*
This highway of love is a frightening, blood-stained road,
there were many a caravan that began... only to fall away.
My pen's ploughing the page with a thirty-lettered team,
love taught to me the thirty-first, beyond speech to say!*
Wealth and things of this world lovers don't bother with:
what that to them really matters is hope, come what may!
In far-off famous Kashmir you will not find one better...
than the sweet, charming women, who are in our land today.

That beautiful woman who before my eyes dresses herself
is so lovely, that even the *houries* of Paradise fade
away.
On my lips my spirit was because of grief about to leave,
remedy you'd not give, selfish maid, your lips my
way!
Don't set your foot down in the street of love until like me
you understand the danger and your life you'll give
away.
Khushul, none will step in for you, no stranger, no friend;
as long as destiny itself isn't seen as being with you
today!

*Note: Khizer is often called: "The Green One" for he was said to have drunk from the Fountain of Immortality and gained Eternal life. He has been identified with Elias, St. George, Phineas, the Angel Gabriel, the companion of Mohammed on a journey which is told in the Koran, viii, 59-8 1, and throughout the literature of Mysticism has appeared to many great seekers who eventually became Perfect Masters. He was said to have accompanied Alexander in his search for the Water of Life (Immortality).
See my 'Khidr in Sufi Poetry' New Humanity Books, 2012.
See Nizami's 2 books on the Life of Alexander.
*The Pashtu alphabet has 30 letters.

What do the unfit or unworthy know of words that are
true?
Better that sugar and spice are words, giving truth to
you?
If you have wisdom and commonsense of words then write:
one true word is worth more, that any gold you may
accrue!
Like going off the path is writing poems without a guide…
one writing a poems without clarity is going nowhere,
too!
An obvious difference is between what is true and untrue:
no comparison is between pearls of paste and pearls,
true!
Although the gnat and the fly, both fly upon the wing…
compare them to hawk or phoenix and they'll never
do.
If words had wings I'd have been able to fly to the sky…
where Jesus the prophet sits, I would now be sitting
too!
These words of Khushal the ordinary man would know;
if blowers of glass, the real worth of real peals ever
knew!

If all people were wise in exactly the same way,
all would be a Luqman, not any difference I say.
If the same for the ruby it would be of no value:
each stones would be from Badakhshan's way!*
If like stones of hail all pearls were the same…
in the houses of all they'd lie, none would stay.
In all of the wilderness it would be worthless,
if sugarcane of India was same reeds… today.
Juicy leaves of summer reeds no ass would eat,
if all leaves of all tress were a betel leaf, I say.
With honour on a king's arm a kite would be,
if it like falcon or hawk was seen as an osprey.
Layla and Majnun's love would be nothing,
if all in the world were as them in every way.
Me, Khushal, has only talked with the truth:
O, if only there was one knowing what I say.

---

*Note: The ruby from Badakhshan is said to be the most valuable in the world and is often compared to the lip of the beloved.

An honest man's actions of all others are better,
for God takes no sides but is friend of one truer!
One whose friendship's only show, heart's thief:
is like a false coin and is shameful, a false-giver.
That, which stinks of evil can't be covered up…
if wrapped in many covers an onion's a stinker!
If you have eyes to look in your heart look now:
look at the world, it is only chaos and disorder!
Be off and by the Indus stand and see it race…
it is cross-currents, like your life, crazy water!
These words you say may be right… so what?
When all are unable to see your actions, ever!
One old or young or born today aren't spared:
the destiny you are given, is the final arbiter!
Khushal, nothing takes one from evil to good:
army of devil, often turns one into a sufferer!

If women of Kashmir are famous for beauty, it's true;
those of China or Tartary for same are famous too…
the sweet Afghan women that these eyes have seen;
that by their conduct, ways, put all to shame is true!
And as for their beauty this is the fact I have noted,
they back from the tribe of Jacob have come through.
They've no need for fragrance of musk or rosewater:
as perfumer's *attar* by prayer five times they're true.
Jewels for forehead, neck, other trinkets, are seen as
contemptible, when their dark ringlets compared to.
And any veils of gold brocade or silk mantles are all
sacrificed; to their snow-white scarves they're true!
Personal charms are excelled by their fine minds…
their hearts are even sweeter than their forms, too!
They are always occupied in private or in seclusion:
not seen in markets, open garments, forms to view.
Through modest they can't look one full in the face:
they don't know abuse or the discipline of the shoe!
Khushal has said about this matter, more or less…
so much is left, suitable or not so, to reveal to you!

The Afghans have gone crazy about positions and
dignities...
but, God preserve me from such troubles and such
plagues.
The gift of discretion is belonging only to the swordsman:
like in the schools is the place one learns the *Koran:*
studies!
With art of prudence not one of them is gifted... not one!
I'm well acquainted with the disposition all of their
stupidities.
If you looked you would see Afghans have a great failing:
they desire from the Mughals dignities and more so
titles!
Of no account... shame and reputation, honour and fame:
but, it is a certainty that they talk about rank, gold,
offices.
Don't look towards the Mughals with such eyes of greed;
even if you're in a habit of doing so due to for other
causes.
Around my waist the trusty Khattaki sword is buckled...
but, never that custom of servitude, in towns and
villages!

I go on remembering dark nights in Aurangzeb's prison,
when through long nights "O God! O God!" my
cries!
If Afghans would only oppose Mughals with swords...
a Mughal each Khattak would lead away by bridle
reins!
Khushal, among Khattaks no council of honour exists:
so, I cannot conceive from which linage were their
ties!

I left and became a dervish... this was my case, my
situation:
in the world all I had was a broken bowl, some rags
on.
Look at those unlucky and see all the good acts they do...
they all want prosperity but it's fleeting, not to rely
upon.
I'll sacrifice myself to that one who sacrificed the world:
but who to gold's sacrificed, to me be a sacrifice in
devotion.
There is nothing in it, a great bustle in an empty shop:
when I meditated on it I saw it was a dream... a
phantom!
While one is laid in a cold grave another sits at home:
three days of mourning and on the fourth... move
on!
And so I escaped, fled from it with hands over ears...
others are wretched, God it's a plague out of all
proportion!
Khushal, what've you to do with others, think of you:
you are tangled up in all of it, it's a calamity, all
rotten!

What's the point of sharpening swords if not to be
striking?
What's the end to hair curled if not to gather some
loving?
Why go on telling me not to notice lovely passing faces?
What's the reason for eyes to be created if not for
looking?
While I drink full glass after glass, shaikh prays, fasts:
isn't is true that each one's made with a different
liking?
You said, "Your lips kisses are like a healing draught!"
As you well know I need that to my own heart be
healing.
Life-blood of my heart you drink, but that is how it is:
why was my heart made, if not for your thirst be
slaking?
Why does one cry so loud about your long black curls?
Doesn't one decide brave such snakes as these…
writhing?
Compared with your lovely face they'll seem as weeds,
those anemones when against your cheeks one is
laying.

There is wine, the flute and the harp and one's beloved:
Khushal, go to rosegarden, in hand your book for
singing!

When longing to see that face, any type of reunion
is enough...
thoughts of such beauty and on cheek, fine down,
is enough!
Kings can wear garments of gold, care that they wear...
on back of the happy beggar one coat well worn,
is enough.
By side of a cool stream sit and watch the waters flow;
as symbol of this passing world this illustration
is enough.
Food, a bellyful's worth; old clothes, two or three suits:
if wise you'll see this as in this world to count on
is enough!
All riches of the world for a greedy one isn't enough...
to the one who is contented of them a single coin
is enough.
I look upon the beautiful face as the pious turn away;
if I am lead to paradise by this, then this one sin
is enough.
So, if I am seen as unfit to look at that one's beauty,
in thoughts and dreams to those eyes gaze upon
is enough.

As a reward both worlds exist for any seeking them:
but for poor Khushal to your eyes look on again
is enough!

If in beauty with red lips, to compare you seek something,
in all Yemen such a carnelian you will never be discovering.
I do not understand whether this mouth is the whole of existence or annihilation, it is a secret none is knowing!
In their thousands they argue their love and friendship: among them I've not one real friend been ever finding.
From this side to that I'm thrown, hitting my sore head: by the times I've become a stone a catapult is slinging.
At first my greatest enemy was my grief for my Friend; now, all I have is One, Who Compassion is bestowing.
One should at first taking this path cut off one's head; when, first this stinking, bloody road one is taking.
Witness the state of the one drowned in a sea of love: the drowning, drowned, of living world know nothing!

That one's on a great quest who seeks God's company:

from that First Day* is brought Grace… for

strengthening.

If you looked at it clearly you'd see the free are captured:

the chains of that One's hair the Masters are

holding!

It looks as though only lovers suffer the injuries of love:

Khushal, with hope Friend comes don't self be

deceiving.

*Note: See note on 'First Day' page 107.

If only there were rose-gardens where together were
you and I…
where roses are shedding petals for to lie together:
you and I!
They can be like saffron, yellow; rosy-pink, sweet-scented:
then through them skipping, one hand in another.
you and I.
If you'd give me your sweet lips to ask some more from…
there would be no other desire but one desire for
you and I.
O if only my grief and pain was a heart hurt due to love,
we'd know no loss while alive but feeling sadder,
you and I.
Let gossiper be confused who fills your days with lies…
lies can find a place to come between us? Never,
you and I!
Khushal, at dawn the sun rises, cock crows its arrival…
needs that we hide tells we have to rise, however,
you and I.

For her lips I asked my sweetheart, but give to me
she wouldn't...
certainly to blame is my rival, for it's a certainty
she wouldn't.
I said to her, "I'll leave your door telling to all my woes,
so... for me pray as I'm leaving," but pray for me
she wouldn't.
Instead of tyranny, I looked for patience from that one;
she showed me that and much more but any mercy
she wouldn't.
I hoped a little, that with one secret glance from far off
she would cure my aching eyes, but to look secretly
she wouldn't.
Hoping to catch a sweet glance from her I'm looking:
it is like a lifetime has passed, but to look at me...
she wouldn't!
I went on hoping as she got sweetly drunk, drinking,
she would a glass of wine give me but obviously
she wouldn't.
From soft, sweet lips she said she'd give me a kiss...
she came closes to me, but one kiss... eventually
she wouldn't.

She plucked a posy of lovely words from her garden…
if by another she had sent it, now to me obviously
she wouldn't.

It isn't she had a hard heart and couldn't please one:
she has a heart that can console, but console me
she wouldn't.

I, Khushal have sought one thing… a pretty maiden:
fortune has much to give… but to make me lucky
she wouldn't!

In grave will be no room for worldly desires or
vanity...
all you'll take is a note of what you did, listed
completely.
A cage isn't worth anything without a parrot shut in it:
the soul could be likened to a parrot and cage a
body!
Be careful that it is not lost or spent without any gain;
each breath, priceless pearls, asked of all you'll
be!
All wasting heritage, throwing priceless pearls aside,
can be thought of as a dumb animal of the field
only.
Pass the graves of all who once were the land's chiefs
and see the thorns and brambles growing there
profusely.
What is done can't be changed no matter your will...
so, why worry in any way and why be doubting
unduly?
What you will take from this world is only a shroud
of eight yards of cloth or nine or ten... if you are
lucky!

My friend, all else you may value you must give up:

beautiful women, wonderful horses, satin robes, finally!

Khushal, get ready now as it's time for on the road:

as caravan moves bells everywhere sound to be ready.

Qasidas...

God has favoured me for He made me out of nothing;
no other creature, but from Adam's seed an offspring.
I am a Muslim of the faith Mohammed my kin gave,
I revere his four companions, what they were doing.*
In the holy Law four schools are thought orthodox…
I believe the Hanafi superior, so follow its teaching.*
God put in my heart love for the wise and real saints
but today's teachers and priests I am not respecting.
I don't go into brothels to drink, gamble or fornicate:
I am no judge or scholar, mind set on money gaining.
The sword is my lot, for by birth I am a true Pathan!
From forebears, my heritage is wealth I am having.
My father and his were all carried to grave bloodied;
but they slew more… their gore everywhere spilling.
Shabaz Khan my father, more kind than Hatim Tai,
heart like a tiger's, sword skill Rustom's bettering.*
He lived by the Law and acted honestly every time;
could not read or write… was always wisely acting.
Grandfather Yahya Khan, how to properly praise?
From head to foot his fine form, beyond describing!
He bettered each rider and out ran each runner too,
such was his body and in bravery he was terrifying.

Great grandfather Ako as chief of the Khattak tribe
was first to make it great, famous as it is still being.
Thirty years have passed since my father was killed:
it was the Yusufzais; may for this, they be burning.
Countless Pathans are with me, but I'm the leader:
I give, take, bind or I lose; if I will it, I'm executing!
Many tribes hate me and one by one them I fight...
they mourned on until they before me were bowing.
Only the Yusufzais placed me in their debt forever:
until today those Akozais honour, firm is standing!
The year the Mughal Aurangzeb was trapping me;
family, tribe were weakened, it was so distressing.*
For years that tyrant Aurangzeb jailed me in India:
I escaped, then safe and sound home was reaching.
Of all who tried to kill me when I was imprisoned
not one is alive, poor or lost, or pain was evading.
Like Joseph escaping Pharaoh's grip, to live again,
I am pure gold whose worth fire is never lessening.
Ashraf Khan, my oldest son, gathered my family...
when into captivity I went, they... were scattering.
I've twenty-four other sons but he is the great one:
God... let all be prosperous, in joy let all be living!

Five, are my grandsons, Afzal is Ashraf's pride…
God prosper him, as future chief him I am seeing.
One brother of mine is a pilgrim on Truth's Path:*
of two others, one is true, the other is often lying.
My and father's home is Malikpur, called Seray…
my kin from here to Lakki, forty leagues are living.
My followers are twenty thousand strong youths;
all my tribe, prepared to out of loyalty be bowing.
I care if Shamsher Khan Tarin is a general now?*
He struts but on the field is a raw turnip, hiding.
How long will he oppose me merely by his rank?
Is it right that a sheep, a lion should be copying?
On Yusufzais a plague, being ruled by a Tarin…
will we soon be seeing, duck on hawk pouncing?
When Shah Jahan was emperor he honoured me,
but now stupidly Aurangzeb all this is reversing.
I grieve so to breathe is hard, I can't be consoled;
bitter wound hurts heart, no doctor it is healing.
These many years how many horsemen worried?
If heart had been stronger would this be passing?
If a hundred years pass, I think this will remain:
if it's still like this, more tragedies are occurring.

As much as Shamsher did through these years,
in just a few months I could have been fulfilling.
These plans and deceits that are his sole skills,
do they befit a man? Work only woman's doing.
Such things need no thought, wisdom: destiny's
eyes are blind to let a woman as Khan be ruling.
His hellish scribbling, his secret notes, letters...
from God's tablet and pen, damnation raining!
I told the truth so all know this... and as I don't
claim to be a poet all praise and blame is ending.

*Notes: Four companions of Prophet Mohammed were the first four Caliphs... Abu Bakr, 'Umar, 'Usman, and 'Ali. Khushal by this declares himself a Sunni.
*There were four interpretations of holy Muslim Law and the Hanafi School was founded by Abu Hanifa.
*Hatim from the tribe of Tai was from pre-Islamic times and renowned for his kindness and generosity.
* Rustom was the Hercules of ancient Persia and is one of the heroes of Firdausi's 'Shah-nama'. This couplet is a chronogram with the letters adding up to the year he was imprisoned by the Mughal emperor Aurangzeb... 1664.
* His brothers talked of here were Tamil Beg who became a mystic known as Faqir Sahib, Mirbaz Khan who stood by him, and Shamsher Khan who plotted with his uncles and the Mughals against him. Mirbaz and Shamsher were half-brothers. Shamsher was appointed governor over the Yusufzais by Aurangzeb, in place of Khushal.

From where to us, has once again been coming the spring
that around the country into garden of flowers, is making?
One can see the anemone and sweet basil, lily and thyme;
jasmine, wild rose, narcissus and pomegranate blossoming.
The wild flowers of spring are everywhere, of every colour;
but, the dark-red tulip above all of them, is predominating.
All the maidens place posies of flowers in their bosoms...
all the young men also in their turbans bouquets are tying.
Musician, come here now... place your bow on your violin:
be bringing out the tone, and also a melody of every string!
And you O winebringer, bring to us full, overflowing cups,
so I'll become overcome with wine's inebriation, instantly!
Youths of Afghanistan have again dyed their hands red...
like the falcon its talons in the blood of its quarry, is dying.
They've made like the rose their bright swords, with gore:
tulip's bed has blossomed, even in summer's heat, blazing!
A'mal Khan, Dar'ya Khan, be they preserved from death...
neither were at fault when the opportunity was occurring.[*]
They dyed red the valley of Khaibar with blood of the foe:
on Karapah[*] they poured out the noise of war and killing.
From Karapah, even to Bujawrr,[*] in plain and mountain...
time after time, as from earthquake, quaked, were shaking.

It is now into the fifth year, since in this neighbourhood, every day the clash of glittering swords one can be hearing. But, since arriving in these parts, I've become a nonentity: either I am despicable, or these people, infamous are being. I cry to them, "Troops, troops!" until I am weary; but, deaf to all, they… not "Die!" nor "Your sacrifice!" are saying.*
When the condition of the Yusufzis became known to me, Aghar was my place to be… Damghar was not existing. The dogs of the Khattaks are far better than the Yusufzais, although in disposition Khattaks are less than dogs being. And… all of the other Afghans, from Kandahar to Attak, both secretly and openly are as one to honour committing. Witness how many battles have been fought on all sides… yet still among the Yusufzis no sense of shame is existing. The first fight was at the higher side of Mount Taturah,* where forty thousand Mughals like chaff were scattering. Their sisters and daughters were captured by the Afghans and their horses, camels, elephants, baggage… everything! The second battle was with Mir Husain in the Doubah:* his head, like that of a venomous snake, we were crushing. Then, after that was the affair at the fort of Noh'shairah,* when from the Mughals my inebriation I was extracting.

And, then was coming Jaswat Singh and Shujaat Khan...
the roots of both, Ae'mal Khan at Ganab up was plucking.
The sixth against Mukarram Khan and Shamsher Khan,
the two, at Khapash, Ae'mal to the winds was scattering.
There are the greatest triumphs that I hold in my memory;
but, smaller ones in every direction, who can be knowing?
Up to the present time, victory has always been with us;
and for the future, our dependence on God, we are placing.
A year has passed since Aurangzeb encamped against us,
disarrayed and perplexed in appearance, in heart suffering.
It has now been year after year that his nobles fall in battle
and his armies swept away; who them, could be counting?
All the treasures of India have been spread out before us...
the reddish-gold *muhurs** in the hills engulfed for taking!
It would never have entered one's head in eighteen guesses
that such events in these parts, would've been happening.
Still, Aurangzeb's malevolence has not one bit diminished;
though his hatred his father's curses, down was drawing.*
For this reason, also, no one can place dependence on him:
he is malignant, perfidious, his word he is always breaking.
In this state of things, no other end can be seen, but this...
either the Mughals be annihilated, or, Afghans are losing.

If this which is now understood, be the turnings of destiny,
if this is the will of the Almighty, the time is now arriving.
Fate is never turning in the same way each time it turns…
now it is favouring the rose, now the thorn it is favouring.
At a period so pregnant with honour and glory as is now,
in what manner are these base, cowardly Yusufazis acting?
There can be no deliverance in anything, except the sword:
Afghans are lost, who other ideas than this are nourishing.
The Afghans are far superior to Mughals with the sword,
if only Afghans were a little circumspect in their thinking.
If all the different tribes would only support one another,
kings in prostration before them would have to be bowing!
But whether it's harmony or strife or if it's folly or wisdom,
the fate of every one in the hands of the Almighty is lying.
Let us see what the Afridis, Mohmands, Shanwaris will do;
for the Mughals encamped at Nagrahur* are now waiting.
I alone, among Afghans, grieve for their honour and name;
while the Yusufazis, at their ease, their fields go on tilling.
They, who are now acting so dishonourably, shamelessly,
will from now on results of their actions be understanding.
In my fallible judgement… death is more preferable to life
when it's impossible with honour, existence to be enjoying.

In this world this one will not always be remaining alive...
but, the memory of Khushal will for a long time be staying!
It was the first day of the Third Sister* in the year of 1675,
that I, while at Barmawul... all these lines were composing.

*Notes: A'mal Khan, Dar'ya Khan... these are the Afridi chiefs, who aided Khushal in his wars with Aurangzeb.
*Karapah: The name of a pass leading from Peshawar to Jalalabad.
*Bujawrr: A small state, held by independent Afghan tribes, north of Peshawar.
*He had gone into the Yusufazi country, to endeavour to persuade that tribe to assist the confederates.
*Mount Taturah: The lofty mountain to the right of the Khaibar Pass, looking from Peshawar and giving name to another Pass, leading to Jalalabad.
*Doubah: A division of the Peshawar district, lying as its name implies, between two rivers, the Landdaey and the Kabul.
*Noh'shairah: A town of the Peshawar district on the northern bank of the Kabul river.
* Muhur: A gold coin of the Mughals that circulated in India from the 16th century.
*Aurangzeb dethroned his father Shah Jahan, whom he confined in prison until his death, which took place seven years after.
* Nagrahur: A small district of Afghanistan at the time, of which Jalalabad was the chief town.
* Third Sister: The fifth month of the Afghan year, so called.

Qit'as...

That one, who never thinks of taking a risk,
or who with one's wealth of gold is a miser...
that one will never be a sultan or a chieftain,
and... will never any land be able to conquer.
And, even if that one is the bravest there is,
will as brave be who is that one's follower?
For the king, the place to be is the throne...
that one must keep it or clang of death hear.
That one who on this earth chooses the bad,
that the earth is covering that one, is better.

One could say that women are like roses
and a rose that is fresh is a joyful vision.
Until the age of twenty she is still fresh,
and, by the time of thirty, is moving on.
When she passes thirty the mind of men
she will leave, her they'll not dwell upon.
And when that one's hair becomes white
does she need to be artistic, be a vision?
Even if she covers herself in gold, will it
compare with beauty… of a young one?
When a beauty is seen by an old man…
from exile his youth comes back… anon.

Discernment, to a gun could be likened:
the game that is in your sight to obtain.
If it is the perfect shot you are needing…
hunter has to be taking the perfect aim.
One should not be afraid to take a shot,
but… know yourself if you begin again.
Below the target be keeping your sight,
and all too high or too low, do not aim.
If any shot then happens to go astray…
I, Khushal… will be staking my name.
And when the time finally comes to die
without flinching accept it, peace gain.

Allow us now to think of my oldest sons
with their works and ways, old and new.
Ashraf Khan knows how to work hard...
how to govern men, to them get through.
Then Sado, he understands their ways...
although to try hard he is not inclined to.
Yahya, he at any work is rushing along...
and so in a moment he is spoiling it, too!
The work of my 'Abid Khan is perfection,
and is a fine leader, through and through.
Now, Khalid Khan, sometimes is good...
but, at other times he can be stupid, too!
Dul, well he is the favourite of his father,
may Abdul live forever... God bless you!
If you look at Baz hard enough in him one
sees some manliness, it can come through.
And Sadr Khan, he was born a champion,
if only God will spare him... for he is true.
Another leader like him is my son Bahram:
even if his heart's confused, I love him too.
In their own ways they are all large men…
may God make them good men, and true!

I have now reached seventy years of age...
as these words I am writing for all of you.
The year is a thousand, ninety-two (1681):
let us see what the heavens will make, too!

One who too many promises are making,
and one who too much goes on borrowing:
with people like these do not make friends
for they are people who are worth nothing.

As Pashtu is my mother-tongue
I will go on singing in Pashtu…
I can see no other Pashtun that
understands it, as well as I do.
There is difference in sweetness
between treacle and sugar… too.
Real honey produced by the bee
is not same as by a wasp. True!
From the same sea comes a real
pearl and a shining stone… too.
Both of them are truly different,
that their worth is also… is true.

With other men do not be at odds…
or, if you have to let the bad be less;
so, if to another you are doing good,
be sure it is a good full of goodness.

The age of Aurangzeb, is this time,

pious beads all men are fingering…

only God its meaning understands,

whether Him others they're serving.

In my house, I have two rebels living,
that are always keeping me so busy...
no matter how I try to hold them back
only when well fed they're quiet, easy.
What they are is not a secret at all...
one my land, one my tongue, you see?
One of poetry wants its share, reward;
the other wants new adventures only.

Of those who died keeping their faith
go to their graves and be respectful…
of all those who live without any faith,
pray that soon they'll of doubt be full.

The time has almost arrived
when in dust lies your body.
Your joints will come apart,
and your flesh carrion only.
About it worms will writhe
or it disappears completely.
But, don't talk of the shell,
that pearl inside let us see!
For a gem is the true pearl,
unique and beyond any fee!

When you die, die in such a way that
somewhere someone will be grieving;
do not be the snake or the scorpion...
whose death relief brings to the living.

Masnavi…

(This excerpt is from Khushal's *masnavi* Farsi-nama)

That One... it is right that One to be praising,
that One... Whose praises every one is singing.
And whether their state high or low should be,
all humans give thanks to One Who is worthy!
All creation is exclaiming that One's Oneness,
from fish in sea to firmament's expansiveness.
Whether, they are infidels or believers so true,
all eventually confess that One's mastery, too.
That One is a King Who is so great, so grand,
the heavens are that One's home, understand?
The earth is its floor... and, the mountains are
like the nails which studding it together... are!
All of these beauties that in the world we see,
are each a description of that One, obviously!
In homage, all of the stones are prostrating...
while all the trees out of respect are standing.
That One made the sun to burn so brightly...
and the moon to shine through night, clearly.
That One made the face of the earth beautiful
by making the flowers bloom, O so colourful!

To the mouth the sense of taste that One gave
and the jaws the strength to chew... to behave.
That One can even make a piece of meat speak
when the fat is spat out, in a hiss, or a squeak!
That One gives to shaikhs will to prayers offer
and gives to a reprobate the will to be a sinner.
That One gives to the rose all of its loveliness
and that One gives to nightingale love, no less.
In flute, that One wonderful music is placing,
and in wine that One places the intoxicating.
That One gives to cock of barnyard its crown,
to peacock that One gives, its colourful train.
To deer that One its perfume gland is giving
and that One to the cat... its civet is giving.
To string of *rebeck* that One gives its song,
to rose-water gives scent for which we long.
That One makes lovely girls, moon-browed,
with those eyes like gazelle's, soft but proud.
That One makes the lover to become so upset
and is inflicting love upon the lover... to get!
That One's making the snow fall or the rain,
that One dries out to dust the meadow again.

That One at first turns bushes into greenery
then is opening flowers on them, for scenery.
Into flowers that One then puts the scent…
then puts colourful petals on them, evident:
it's so one can adore them tending a garden
and the hillsides with flowers covering them.
And, all trees of the fields and orchards too,
all of the small and the wide and the tall too,
to all, that One a different fruit has given…
and all that One a different taste has given.
That One covers vines with grape-clusters
makes the red and white sweet, in bunches.
The bounty of that One, it rains equally…
upon the colocynth and the apple, equally!
so as the beautiful rose forth is blossoming
like all thorns are growing out… prickling!
From the bountiful table of that One all eat,
to sit at that full table they do not compete:
even the sinner is eating until he is full at it
beside the pious one who also at it does sit!
That One, kings upon thrones is placing…
that One when their time comes, is taking!

And if that One's wishing to pardon Lucifer
none can say to that One, "Do not bother!"
If that One is casting into flame somebody
there is not one who can protest… nobody!
If kingship is lying in being independent…
that One's the greatest thing, Independent!
Kingdom of that One's never a low knowing,
there's none above One Who's ever existing!

WORKS PUBLISHED OR SOON TO BE PUBLISHED BY NEW HUMANITY BOOKS

MOST 6" X 9" PAPERBACKS PERFECTBOUND

Many of the books below are already in KINDLE

TRANSLATIONS

(NOTE: All translations by Paul Smith are in clear, modern English and in the correct rhyme-structure of the originals and as close to the true meaning as possible.)

DIVAN OF HAFIZ
Revised Translation & Introduction by Paul Smith
This is a completely revised one volume edition of the only modern, poetic version of Hafiz's masterpiece of 791 *ghazals, masnavis, rubais* and other poems/songs. The spiritual and historical and human content is here in understandable, beautiful poetry: the correct rhyme-structure has been achieved, without intruding, in readable (and singable) English.
In the Introduction of 70 pages his life story is told in greater detail than any where else; his spirituality is explored, his influence on the life, poetry and art of the East and the West, the form and function of his poetry, and the use of his book as a worldly guide and spiritual oracle. His Book, like the *I Ching*, is one of the world's Great Oracles. Included are notes to most poems, glossary and selected bibliography and two indexes. First published in a two-volume hardback limited edition in 1986 the book quickly went out of print. 542 pages.

PERSIAN AND HAFIZ SCHOLARS AND ACADEMICS WHO HAVE COMMENTED ON PAUL SMITH'S FIRST VERSION OF HAFIZ'S *'DIVAN'*.
"It is not a joke... the English version of ALL the *ghazals* of Hafiz is a great feat and of paramount importance. I am astonished. If he comes to Iran I will kiss the fingertips that wrote such a masterpiece inspired by the Creator of all and I will lay down my head at his feet out of respect."
Dr. Mir Mohammad Taghavi (Dr. of Literature) Tehran.
"I have never seen such a good translation and I would like to write a book in Farsi and introduce his Introduction to Iranians." Mr B. Khorramshai, Academy of Philosophy, Tehran.
"Superb translations. 99% Hafiz 1% Paul Smith."Ali Akbar Shapurzman, translator of many mystical works in English to Persian and knower of Hafiz's *Divan* off by heart.

"I was very impressed with the beauty of these books." Dr. R.K. Barz. Faculty of Asian Studies, Australian National University.
"Smith has probably put together the greatest collection of literary facts and history concerning Hafiz." Daniel Ladinsky (Penguin Books author of poems inspired by Hafiz).

HAFIZ – THE ORACLE
(For Lovers, Seekers, Pilgrims, and the God-Intoxicated).
Translation & Introduction & Interpretations by Paul Smith.
Hafiz's Divan has been used as an Oracle successfully by millions of people from all walks of life for the past 600 years. The practice of interpreting his poems has been going on in Iran for many centuries. Here are almost four hundred of his *ghazals* with insightful and clear interpretations by Paul Smith plus an Introduction that includes his life, poetry, spirituality and the history of the use of his book as one of the world's great Oracles. The correct rhyme-structure has been kept as well as the beauty and meaning of these beautiful, mystical poems. 441 pages

HAFIZ OF SHIRAZ.
The Life, Poetry and Times of the Immortal Persian Poet.
Three Volumes
by Paul Smith
Told through the eyes of Hafiz's lifelong friend and student Muhammad Gulandam, this long, historical novel based on ten years of research and writing covers Hafiz's life from the age of eight in 1328 when his father dies and he goes to live with his Uncle Sadi until after his death in 1392. Shiraz is under siege by the tyrant Mubariz and Hafiz's friend the king, Abu Ishak, is on the brink of madness and despair. Along the way Hafiz falls in love with his muse the beautiful Nabat, meets his Spiritual Master, marries and has a son. He teaches at University and befriends the liberated princess Jahan Khatun(Iran's greatest female poet) after being a student of the outrageous poet/jester Obeyd Zakani. He experiences kingdoms rise and fall, the people of his beloved city throwing out dictators, and the wrath of the false Sufi and black magician Shaikh Ali Kolah. This is a majestic love story on a level of great love, beauty and consciousness, full of action and adventure, immortal poetry and song, bravery and betrayal and destiny. After the bloodthirsty tyrant Mubariz takes control in Shiraz closing the winehouses, imprisoning Hafiz's friend the poet, Princess Jahan and forcing Obeyd Zakani to flee for his life. Abu Ishak is executed and the false Sufi Ali Kolah is now in control of religious morals. Eventually Mubariz's son Shah Shuja takes control but tragedy strikes Hafiz and Jahan, and Nabat

must suffer separation. Kingdoms rise and fall through treachery and wars but through it all the songs/*ghazals* of Hafiz and his minstrel friends help the brave Shirazis to carry on until finally Hafiz gives his Master Attar an ultimatum after 40 years of devotion... God-Realisation or else! Over 1900 pages.

PIERCING PEARLS: THE COMPLETE ANTHOLOGY OF PERSIAN POETRY (Court, Sufi, Dervish, Satirical, Ribald, Prison & Social Poetry from the 9th to the 20th century.) Volume One
Translations, Introduction and Notes by Paul Smith
This 2 volume anthology is the largest anthology of Persian Poetry ever published. The introduction contains a history and explanation of all the forms used by the poets, a short history of the Persian language, Sufism in Persian Poetry & a Glossary of Sufi & Dervish Symbols plus a Selected Bibliography.
With each selection of a particular poet is a brief biography plus a list of further reading. The correct rhyme-structure has been kept as well as the beauty and meaning of these beautiful, often mystical poems.
THE POETS... Volume One 9th to the 13th Century.
Abbas of Merv page 29, Hanzalah 30, Firuz 31, Abu Salik 32, Abu Shakur 33, Junaidi, 35, Shahid, 36, Rudaki 38, Agachi 48, Rabi'a Balkhi 49, Khusravani 57, Manjik 58, Daqiqi 60, Mantiki 67, Umarah 69, Kisa'i 70, Firdausi 74, Baba Tahir 83, Farrukhi 88, Asjadi 100, Manuchirhri 101, Gurgani 106, Unsuri 110, Abu Said 116, Ibn Sina 123, Baba Kuhi 125, Nasir-i-Khusraw 127, Asadi 131, Azraqi 137, Qatran 140, Ansari 145, Al-Ghazali 147, Mas'ud Sad 149, Mu'izzi 159, Hamadani 168, Omar Khayyam 172, Sana'i 174, Sabir 189, Mahsati 182, Jabali 193, Vatvat 197, Anvari 201, Falaki 212, Khaqani 229, Zahir 242, Nizami 252, Ruzbihan 286, Baghdadi 288, 'Attar 290, Auhad ud-din Kermani 315, Kamal ad-din 320, Hamavi 325, Baba Afzal 328, Rumi 331, Imami 389, Hamgar 390, Sadi 395, Iraki 439, Humam 452, Amir Khusraw 457, Hasan Dilhavi 473, Simnani 475, Auhadi 478, Ibn Yamin 484, Khaju 490. Pages... 532

PIERCING PEARLS: THE COMPLETE ANTHOLOGY OF PERSIAN POETRY (Court, Sufi, Dervish, Satirical, Ribald, Prison & Social Poetry from the 9th to the 20th century.) Vol. Two
Translations, Introduction and Notes by Paul Smith
This 2 volume anthology is the largest anthology of Persian Poetry ever published. The introduction contains a history and explanation of all the forms used by the poets, a short history of the Persian language, Sufism in Persian Poetry & a Glossary of Sufi & Dervish Symbols plus a Selected

Bibliography. Included with each selection of a particular poet is a brief biography plus a list of further reading. The rhyme-structure has been kept as well as the beauty and meaning of these beautiful, often mystical poems. THE POETS: Volume Two… 14th Century to Modern Times …Obeyd Zakani page 27, Emad 63, Salman 76, Shahin 84, Hafiz 105, Ruh Attar 173, Haydar 189, Azad 203, Junaid Shirazi 206, Jahan Khatun 211, Shah Shuja 244, Kamal 249, Maghribi 253, Bushaq 263, Kasim Anwar 276, Shah Ni'tmu'llah 284, Jami 291, Fighani 309, Babur 314, Humayan 317, Kamran 319, Ghazali 321, Kahi 323, Akbar 325, Urfi 326, Hayati 331, Ulfati 332, Dara Shikoh 333, Sarmad 336, Sa'ib 343, Nasir Ali 347, Makhfi 348, Bedil 358, Mushtaq 366, Hatif 370, Tahirah 377, Iqbal 392, Parvin 398, Khalili 423, Rahi 426, Simin 428. Pages 490.

DIVAN OF SADI: His Mystical Love-Poetry.
Translation & Introduction by Paul Smith
Sadi's mystical love poetry, his *ghazals*, although almost unknown in the West, are loved by his fellow-countrymen almost as much as those of Hafiz whom he greatly influenced. Here for the first time in English they can be read in all their beauty and power and spirit. The correct rhyme-structure has been kept as well as the beauty and meaning of these beautiful, mystical poems. ALL of the wonderful 603 *ghazals* from Sadi's *Badayi* and *Tayyibat* have been translated in clear, modern, meaningful, correct-rhyming English. Included is an Introduction containing The Life of Sadi, his Poetry and his influence on the East and the West and on the form and meaning of the *ghazal*. 421 pages.

RUBA'IYAT OF SADI
Translation & Introduction by Paul Smith
Here for the first time in beautiful English are eighty-eight of Sadi's wonderful short poems or *ruba'is* in the correct rhyme-structure and with all the meanings. Some are mystical others romantic, satirical and humourous and others critical of the selfishness of the time, of all time. As fresh today as they were when they were composed some 800 years ago. Included is an Introduction containing The Life of Sadi, his Poetry and his influence on the East and the West and a history of the form of the *ruba'i* and examples by its greatest exponents. The correct rhyme-structure has been kept as well as the beauty and meaning of these beautiful, mystical poems. 133 pages.

WINE, BLOOD & ROSES: ANTHOLOGY OF TURKISH POETS
Sufi, Dervish, Divan, Court & Folk Poetry from the 14th – 20th Century
Translations, Introductions, Notes etc., by Paul Smith
Introduction includes chapters on... The Turkish Language, Turkish Poetry, The Ghazal in Turkish Poetry, The Roba'i in Turkish Poetry, The Mesnevi in Turkish Poetry, The Qasida in Turkish Poetry and a Glossary. Included with each selection of a particular poet is a brief biography plus a list of further reading. The correct rhyme-structure has been kept as well as the beauty and meaning of these beautiful, often mystical poems.
THE POETS...Sultan Valad page 27, Yunus Emre 36, Kadi Burhan-ud-din 60, Nesimi 70, Ahmedi 87, Sheykhi 93, Ahmed Pasha 96, Mihri 100, Zeyneb 108, Jem 110, Necati 115, Zati 128, Pir Sultan 133, Khayali 140, Fuzuli 150, Baqi 172, Huda'i 188, Nef'i 190, Yahya 200, Haleti 208, Na'ili 216, Niyazi 221, Nabi 229, Nedim 235, Fitnet 243, Galib 250, Esrar Dede 261, Leyla Khanim 265, Veysel 268. Pages 273.

OBEYD ZAKANI: THE DERVISH JOKER.
A Selection of his Poetry, Prose, Satire, Jokes and Ribaldry.
Translation & Introduction by Paul Smith
Obeyd Zakani is an important a figure in Persian and Sufi literature and poetry. His satire, humorous stories, ribald and obscene poems, social commentary, mystical *ghazals*, prose, *ruba'is* and his famous epic *qasida* 'Mouse & Cat' are popular today and are more relevant than ever. He is considered to be one of the world's greatest satirist and social-commentator whose life and mystical poems had a great influence on his student and friend Hafiz and many others. This is the largest selection of his work available in English. The correct rhyme-structure has been kept as well as the beauty and meaning of these beautiful, sometimes mystical poems. 284 pages.

OBEYD ZAKANI'S > MOUSE & CAT ^ ^
(The Ultimate Edition)
Translation & Introduction etc by Paul Smith
Obeyd Zakani's *Mouse & Cat* is a satirical, epic fable in the poetic form of the *qasida* that was influential at the time it was composed (14th C.) and has remained so for the past 600 years. It is more than just a story for children (that some say brought about the cartoon of Tom & Jerry)... it is a story of the stupidity of the false power of those in power and a warning to all that such blind ambition always leads to destruction at the hands of one even more powerful. Here is a beautiful, poetic translation keeping to the

correct form of the famous *qasida* illustrated with unique Persian miniatures.
Included is a long Introduction on The Life, Times and Writings of Obeyd Zakani. Appendixes include… Examples of all other translations into English; Obeyd performs *Mouse & Cat* for a young prince (from the Novel/Biog. *Hafiz of Shiraz*); a 1940's Illustrated Persian edition of *Mouse & Cat*, The Corrected Persian Text of *Mouse & Cat* and The First Complete Translation into literal English in 1906. Selected Bibliography. 169 pages.

THE GHAZAL: A WORLD ANTHOLOGY
Translations, Introductions, Notes, Etc. by Paul Smith
Introduction includes…The Ghazal in Arabic, Persian, Turkish, Urdu, Punjabi, Pushtu, Sindhi, Kashmiri & English Poetry. Glossary.
Included with each selection of a particular poet is a brief biography plus a list of further reading. The correct rhyme-structure has been kept as well as the beauty and meaning of these beautiful, often mystical poems.
THE POETS…Hazrat Ali page 27, Rabi'a of Basra 28, Dhu'l-Nun 32, Mansur al-Hallaj 34, Khusravani 37, Shahid 38, Manjik 39, Rudaki 40, Rabi'a Balkhi 43, Daqiqi 47, Kisa'i 49, Firdausi 51, Unsuri 53, Baba Kuhi 56, Qatran 57, Mas'ud Sa'd 59, Mu'izzi 62, Sana'i 64, Sabir 67, Falaki 69, Jabali 72, Vatvat 74, Anvari 75, Khaqani 77, Nizami 80, 'Attar 84, Kamal ud-din 96, Ibn al-Farid 98, Ibn 'Arabi 101, Rumi 106, Imami 121, Sadi 122, Hamgar 154, Iraki 156, Humam 163, Yunus Emre 165, Amir Khusraw 177, Hasan Dilhavi 188, Auhadi 190, Ibn Yamin 192, Khaju 193, Obeyd Zakani 199, Emad 208, Salman 218, Azad 221, Hafiz 224, Ruh Attar 264, Haydar 269, Junaid Shirazi 274, Kadi Burhan-ud-din 278, Jahan Khatun 281, Kamal 302, Maghribi 305, Nesimi 314, Bushaq 325, Shah Ni'matu'llah 337, Ahmedi 339, Sheykhi 343, Kasim Anwar 345, Jami 350, Baba Fighani 363, Babur 368, Ahmed Pasha 370, Mihri 372, Zeyneb 377, Jem 379, Necati 382, Zati 386, Pir Sultan 390, Khayali 394, Kamran 401, Fuzuli 402, Huda'i 412, Kahi 414, Baqi 416, Urfi 422, Yahya 425, Qutub Shah 428, Mirza 431, Haleti 442, Sa'ib 444. Na'ili 446, Niyazi 449. Khushal 452, Ashraf Khan 467, Makhfi 473, Nabi 507, Bedil 510, Abdul-Khadir 514, Rahman Baba 521, Khwaja Mohammad 536, Hamid 547, Wali 557, Nedim 561, Mushtaq 565, Ali Haider 567, Fitnet 568, Sauda 573, Dard 575, Ahmad Shah 578, Shaida 486, Nazir 592, Mir 599, Sachal Sarmast 606, Galib 611, Esrar Dede 618, Lelya Khanim 620, Mahmud Gami 621, Aatish 623, Zauq 627, Ghalib 630, Momin 636, Tahirah 639, Shad 647, Iqbal 651, Ashgar 657, Mahjoor 660, Jigar 613, Huma 669, Veysel 695, Firaq 699, Josh 704, Parvin 707, Rahi 713, Faiz 715, Simin 717, Paul 719. Pages 758.

NIZAMI: THE TREASURY OF MYSTERIES
Translation & Introduction by Paul Smith
"The Makhzanol Asrar (The Treasury of Mysteries), the most beautiful mystic poem in the Persian language, has both perfection of language and grandeur of thought. Every line of his Treasury of Mysteries is a living witness to his absolute certainty that piety, devotion, humility and self-forgetfulness are the corner stones of total annihilation, which in turn is necessary for unification with God and the foundation of the edifice of eternal life." G. H. Darab. Senior lecturer in Persian. University of London. Paul Smith has kept to the correct rhyme-structure while retaining the meaning and beauty of the original in simple, understandable, poetic English. He has written a long Introduction on the Life of Nizami and chapters on each of his books of poetry. Bibliography. 245 pages.

NIZAMI: LAYLA AND MAJNUN
Translation & Introduction by Paul Smith
It is impossible to underestimate the effect of Nizami's 'Layla and Majnun' on the world over the past 800 years. Many poets throughout this period have copied or been influenced by his story of the young lovers. Many Master-Poets besides Ibn Arabi, Attar, Rumi, Sadi, Hafiz and Jami have quoted from him or like him have used the story of the desperate lovers to illustrate how human love can be transformed into divine love through separation and longing. It is said that no one has painted a more perfect picture of women in Persian Literature than Nizami.
Paul Smith has kept to the correct rhyme-structure of this long *masnavi* epic poem, while retaining the beauty of the poetry, the mystical meaning and simplicity of the form. He has included a long Introduction on his life and chapters on all of the works of this great Master/Poet. Selected Bibliography. 216 pages.

UNITY IN DIVERSITY: Anthology of Sufi and Dervish Poets of the Indian Sub-Continent
Translations, Introductions, Notes, Etc. by Paul Smith
Introduction includes...Sufis & Dervishes: Their Art and Use of Poetry; Glossary of Sufi and Dervish Symbols; The Main Forms in Persian, Hindi, Urdu, Punjabi, Sindhi & Kashmiri Sufi & Dervish Poetry of the Indian Sub-Continent. Included with each selection of a particular poet is a brief biography plus a list of further reading. The correct rhyme-structure has been kept as well as the beauty and meaning of these beautiful, mystical poems.

THE POETS... Baba Farid page 37, Amir Khusraw 45, Hasan Dihlavi 57, Lalla Ded 59, Kabir 62, Qutub Shah 77, Dara Shikoh 80, Sarmad 83, Sultan Bahu 93, Nasir Ali 98, Makhfi 100, Wali 138, Bulleh Shah 143, Shah Latif 151, Ali Haider 160, Sauda 164, Dard 168, Nazir 173, Mir 189, Sachal Sarmast 204, Aatish 211, Zauq 217, Dabir 221, Anees 223, Hali 225, Farid 227, Shad 230, Iqbal 236, Inayat Khan 249, Asghar 266, Jigar 269, Huma 275, Firaq 307, Josh 312. Pages... 325.

RUBA'IYAT OF RUMI
Translation & Introduction and Notes by Paul Smith
Here are 330 wonderful *ruba'is* of the great Spiritual Master of the 13th century, who has become today the most popular poet in the world, Jelal ad-din Rumi: they are powerful, spiritual and full of joy, bliss and understanding. Unlike those of Omar Khayyam's these are poems composed by a soul before and *after* gaining God-realisation. Included in the Introduction is the life of Rumi and a history of the *ruba'i* and examples by its greatest exponents. Selected Bibliography. The correct rhyme-structure has been kept as well as the beauty and meaning of these immortal four-line poems. 368 pages.

RUMI: SELECTED POEMS
Translation, Introduction & Notes by Paul Smith
Included in the Introduction is the life of Rumi and chapters on the *ruba'i*, the *ghazal*, the *masnavi and the qasida*. Selected Bibliography. Glossary. The correct rhyme-structure has been kept as well as the beauty and meaning of these immortal poems of this most popular Perfect Spiritual Master and Master Poet. 217 pages.

THE MASNAVI: A WORLD ANTHOLOGY
Translations, Introduction and Notes by Paul Smith
Introduction includes... Article on the masnavi in various languages. With each selection of a particular poet is a brief biography plus a list of further reading. The correct rhyme-structure has been kept as well as the beauty and meaning of these beautiful, often mystical poems.
THE POETS...Abu Shakur page 13, Rabi'a Balkhi 15, Daqiqi 21, Firdausi 26, Gurgani 35, Nasir-i-Khusraw 39, Asadi 43, Sana'i 44, Khaqani 49, Zahir 52, Nizami 55, 'Attar 83, Rumi 91, Sadi 128, Sultan Valad 135, Yunus Emre 140, Amir Khusraw 144, Auhadi 149, Khaju 152, Obeyd Zakani 152, Shahin 157, Hafiz 178, Ruh Attar 192, Kasim Anwar 196, Shah Ni'tmu'llah 200, Jami 207, Fuzuli 207, Mir 210, Tahirah 219, Iqbal 225, Inayat Khan 231, Parvin 248, Paul 257. 268 pages.

HAFIZ'S FRIEND, JAHAN KHATUN: The Persian Princess Dervish Poet...A Selection of Poems from her *Divan*
Translated by Paul Smith and Rezvaneh Pashai.

Daughter of the king of one of Shiraz's most turbulent times (8th century A.H. 14th century A.D.) ... Masud Shah; pupil and lifelong friend of the world's greatest mystical, lyric poet, Hafiz of Shiraz; the object of crazed desire by (among others) Iran's greatest satirist, the obscene, outrageous, visionary poet Obeyd Zakani; lover, then wife of womaniser Amin al-Din, a minister of one of Persia's most loved, debauched and tragic rulers Abu Ishak; imprisoned for twenty years under the Muzaffarids while her young daughter mysteriously died; open-minded and scandalous, one of Iran's first feminists ... the beautiful, petite princess who abdicated her royalty twice; one of Iran's greatest classical lyric poets; a prolific, profound, infamous female Persian poet...one of the greatest mystical love poets of all time whose *Divan* is four times the size of Hafiz's. The correct rhyme-structure is kept as well as the beauty and meaning of these beautiful, often mystical poems. 191 pages.

KABIR: SEVEN HUNDRED SAYINGS (SAKHIS).
Translation & Introduction by Paul Smith

'Here are wonderful words of wisdom from one of the wisest of the wise. Here are lines of love from a Master of Divine Love, and a human being who has lived as all human beings should live, with compassion, honesty and courage. If you want the Truth, no holds barred, it is here, but as we're told; truth is dangerous! These poems change people. You will not be the same! As Kabir says. "Wake up sleepy head!" ' From the Introduction which includes a Glossary & Selected Bibliography. 188 pages.

PRINCESSES, SUFIS, DERVISHES, MARTYRS & FEMINISTS: NINE GREAT WOMEN POETS OF THE EAST
A Selection of the Poetry of Rabi'a of Basra, Rabi'a of Balkh, Mahsati, Lalla Ded, Jahan Khatun, Makhfi, Tahirah, Hayati and Parvin.
Introduction & Translations by Paul Smith

Rabi'a of Basra (d. 801) is considered one of the greatest Saints and founders of Sufism and composed powerful spiritual verse in Arabic.
Rabi'a of Balkh (10th c.) was the princess of Afghanistan whose love for a slave of her father the king caused her downfall at the hands of her mad brother... she wrote many of her poems to her beloved in her own blood on the walls of the prison where he tortured her to death.
Mahsati (12th century) was the liberated court poet of Sultan Sanjar who knew Nizami, Omar Khayyam and other poets of that time. Like Omar she

only composed in the *ruba'i* form that she revolutionized with her often scandalous verse.

Lalla Ded (1320-1392) is the famous female poet/saint from Kashmir who lived at *exactly* the same time as Hafiz of Shiraz (1320-1392). Her *vakhs* (poem/sayings) are sung even today in Kashmir. She was married at a young age but the marriage was a failure and she walked out at the age of twenty-four. It must have taken a lot of courage on her part to walk around unclothed as she did. She was treated with contempt by some and much reverence by others, seeing her as a saint and eventually as God-realized. Her two hundred *vakhs* are some of the oldest examples of Kashmiri written. She was a bridge between Hindu mysticism and Sufism.

Jahan Khatun (1326-1416) was a beautiful, liberated princess in Shiraz and a friend and pupil of the great Hafiz... her *Divan* is four times the size of his. She spent 20 years in prison where her daughter died. Her *ghazals, ruba'is* and other fine poems put her in the highest rung of Persian Poets.

Makhfi or Zebunissa (1638-1702) was the daughter of the fundamentalist Emperor of India Aurangzeb and was eventually imprisoned by him and tortured to death for her Sufi views and conspiring with a brother to overthrow him. Her over 550 *ghazals* and *ruba'is* in classical Persian are deep, powerful, spiritual and at times heartbreaking.

Tahirah... (1817-1853). Tahirah was a beautiful and intelligent woman who led a short and stormy life. She became a devotee of the Bab, who from Shiraz had given his prophetic message that would later appear in the form of Baha-ul-lah, the founder of the Baha'is. She was not only a poet but also wrote prose, knew literature, religious laws and interpretations of the *Koran* and lectured... very unusual for a woman of that time and previous times in Iran. She was thirty-six when sentenced to death after the Shah was assassinated leading to a massacre of the Baha'is.

Hayati (mid 18th century - early 19th century). Bibi Hayati Kermani was born into a Sufi family in the Kerman province of Persia. She was raised by her brother, who guided her in the early stages of her spiritual life. When she was older she was initiated into the Ni'matullahi Sufi order by the Sufi Master Nur 'Ali Shah, who she was later to marry. At the request of her husband Hayati quickly composed her poetry and in her lifetime became well-known for her passionate, mystical poems that combine her great love for her husband with her devotion to Hazrat 'Ali and union with God.

Parvin... (1907-1941). Parvin E'tesami was one of Iran's greatest female poets. She learned Arabic and Persian literature from her father. She composed her first poems at eight and knew most Iranian poets by the time she was eleven, having a remarkable memory. She received a Medal of Art and Culture in 1936. Her poems had mainly social or mystical subjects, often being about the tyranny of the rich and the rights of the poor and the downtrodden and the role of women. She died in 1941 from Typhoid. The correct rhyme-structure has been kept as well as the beauty and meaning of these beautiful, sometimes mystical poems. Pages 367.

SHAH LATIF: SELECTED POEMS
Translation & Introduction by Paul Smith
Shah Abdul Latif (1689-1752) was a Sufi Master and is considered by many to be the greatest poet of the Sindhi language. His book of poetry is called the *Risalo*. His shrine is located in Bhit and attracts hundreds of pilgrims every day. He is the most famous Sindhi poet and Sufi. He was not just adored for poetry, people from far and near respected and loved him as a Spiritual Master. He composed *dohas* (self-contained strict-rhyming couplets popular with poet-saints of India like Kabir, Surdas, Tukaram) and freed it from the chain of two lines, extending it to even five or six couplets, often with irregular rhyme structures. He also introduced one more string to the *tambura,* a drone instrument and founded a new tradition in music based on the synthesis of high art and folk art. He told the basic principles of Sufism in his poetry, often using folktales about human love such as that of Sasui and Punhu, becoming a bridge to Divine Love. 172 pages

LALLA DED: SELECTED POEMS
Translation & Introduction by Paul Smith
Lalla Ded is the famous female poet/saint from Kashmir who lived at *exactly* the same time as Hafiz of Shiraz (1320-1392). Her *vakhs* (poem/sayings) are sung even today in Kashmir. She was married at a young age but the marriage was a failure and she walked out at the age of twenty-four. She became a disciple of Siddha Srikanth. It must have taken a lot of courage on her part to walk out of a marriage and to walk around unclothed as she did. She was treated with contempt by some and much reverence by others, seeing her as a saint and eventually as God-realized. Her two hundred *vakhs* are some of the oldest examples of Kashmiri written. She was a bridge between Hindu mysticism and Sufism. Her poems are more influential today than ever, not only in Kashmir but around the world. Here are 134 poems with correct form and meaning. 140 pages.

BULLEH SHAH: SELECTED POEMS
Translation & Introduction by Paul Smith
Bulleh Shah (1680-1758) was a Sufi poet who composed in Punjabi and settled in Kasur, now in Pakistan. His Spiritual Master was Shah Inayat. The poetic form Bulleh Shah is called the *Kafi*, a style of Punjabi poetry

used not only by the Sufis of Sindh and Punjab, but also by Sikh gurus. His poetry and philosophy strongly criticizes the Islamic religious orthodoxy of his day. His time was marked with communal strife between Muslims and Sikhs. But in that age Bulleh Shah was a beacon of hope and peace for the citizens of Punjab. Several of his songs or *kafis* are regarded as an integral part of the traditional repertoire of *qawwali,* the musical genre that represents the devotional music of the Sufis. The correct rhyme-structure has been kept as well as the beauty and meaning of these poems. 141 pages.

NIZAMI: MAXIMS
Translation & Introduction Paul Smith
Nizami (d. 1208) is a true Sufi Master Poet who is most famous for his six books in *masnavi* form: *The Treasury of the Mysteries, Layla and Majnun, Khrosrau and Shirin, The Seven Portraits* and his two books on Alexander. He also composed a *Divan* of approximately 20,000 couplets mostly in *ghazals* and *ruba'is…* tragically only 200 couplets survive. His influence on Attar, Rumi, Sadi, Hafiz, Jami, Shakespeare and others that followed was profound. Included in the Introduction… on the Life, Times & Poetry of Nizami includes chapters on his six *masnavis* and his *Divan,* and on the various forms of poetry he used and a Selected Bibliography. The correct rhyme-structure has been kept as well as the beauty and meaning of these wonderful two-line maxims that are not only profound, but also simple. Illustrated 214 pages.

KHIDR IN SUFI POETRY: A SELECTION
Translation & Introduction by Paul Smith
Khidr (Khizer, Khadir) is often called: "The Green One" for he was said to have drunk from the Fountain of Immortality and gained Eternal life. He has been identified with Elias, St. George, Phineas, the Angel Gabriel, the companion of Mohammed on a journey which is told in the *Koran,* viii, 59-8 1, and throughout the literature of Mysticism has appeared to many great seekers who eventually became Perfect Masters. Here are poems by many great Sufi Master Poets who have composed poems in Persian, Turkish, Pashtu, Urdu and English in which he is invoked or appears: Ansari, Anvari, Khaqani, Mu'in, Nizami, 'Attar, Baba Afzal, Rumi, Sadi, Yunus Emre, Shabistari, Amir Khusrau, Obeyd Zakani, Emad Kermani, Hafiz, Ruh Attar, Haydar, Jahan Khatun, Ahmedi, Zeyneb, Necati, Khushal, Makhfi, Rahman Baba, Khwaja Mohammad, Niyazi, Wali, Dard, Zauq, Ghalib, Dagh, Iqbal, Paul. The correct rhyme-structure has been kept as well as the beauty and meaning of these poems in various forms. Introduction on 'Who is Khidr'… Three Appendixes. Illustrated. 267 pages.

ADAM: THE FIRST PERFECT MASTER AND POET
by Paul Smith
In a series of conversations between a Master and devotees over a number of days and nights this is a long-overdue exploration and discovery and appreciation of the real spiritual status of Adam, the first God-realized human being and the first poet. Using poetry and texts of the greatest Sufi and other mystical poets this first Perfect Master's life and role is revealed and praised. The poets and Spiritual Masters include Adam Himself, Hafiz, Ibn 'Arabi, Shahin of Shiraz, 'Iraqi, Jili, Hallaj, Khushal Khan Khattak, Rumi, Ansari, Nizami, Surawadi, Mu'in ud-din Chishti, Sadi, Ibn al-Farid and Paul. The correct rhyme-structure has been kept as well as the beauty and meaning of these poems in various forms. 185 pages.

MODERN SUFI POETRY: A SELECTION
Translations & Introduction by Paul Smith
Here is one of the few anthologies of modern Sufi poetry of poets that have made a lasting impression on the present times. All the poets and Poet/Masters in this collection either died or were born in the 20th century. Most of the poets in this collection composed in the forms of earlier Sufi poets: *ghazal, ruba'i, qasida, kafi, masnavi*. Introduction: Sufis & Dervishes: Their Art and Use of Poetry, The Main Forms in Sufi and Dervish Poetry. THE POETS: Hali 47, Farid 51, Shad 57, Khusrawi 66, Iqbal 70, Munis 'Ali Shah 90, Inayat Khan 97, Asghar 122, Jigar 128, Khadim 140, Huma 151, Veysel 168, Firaq 175, Josh 185, Francis Brabazon 194, Khalili 207, Nurbaksh 214, Paul 217. Pages 249

LIFE, TIMES & POETRY OF NIZAMI
Paul Smith
Nizami (d. 1208) is a true Sufi Master Poet who is most famous for his six books in *masnavi* form: *The Treasury of the Mysteries, Layla and Majnun, Khosrau and Shirin, The Seven Portraits* and his two books on Alexander. He also composed a *Divan* of approximately 20,000 couplets mostly in *ghazals* and *ruba'is*... tragically only 200 couplets survive. His influence on Attar, Rumi, Sadi, Hafiz and Jami and all others that followed was profound. Here a number of his *ghazals* and *ruba'is* and a *qasida* translated into English and a good selection from his *masnavis*. This book is on The Life and Times and Poetry of Nizami and on the various forms of poetry he used and the reason why he composed his major works and their effect on the times and our time. Selected Bibliography. The correct rhyme-structure

has been kept as well as the beauty and meaning of the selected beautiful, mystical poems. 97 pages.

RABI'A OF BASRA: SELECTED POEMS
Translation by Paul Smith

RABI'A OF BASRA (717-801). Throughout her life, her Love of God, poverty and self-denial did not waver. She did not possess much other than a broken jug, a rush mat and a brick, which she used as a pillow. She spent nights in prayer and contemplation, chiding herself if she slept because it took her away from her active Love of God. As her fame grew she had many disciples. More interesting than her asceticism is the actual concept of Divine Love that Rabi'a introduced. She was the first to introduce the idea that God should be loved for God's own sake, not out of fear -- as earlier Sufis had done. She taught that repentance was a gift from God as none could repent unless God had already accepted him and given this gift of repentance. She had a high ideal, worshipping God neither from fear of Hell nor from hope of Paradise, for she saw such self-interest as unworthy of God's servants; emotions like fear and hope were like veils. She is widely considered the most important of the early Sufi poets. Here are most of the small number of her poems that survive, in the forms in which they were composed, also an introduction on her life and times and a chapter on Sufi poetry. 100 pages.

SATIRICAL PROSE OF OBEYD ZAKANI
Translation and Introduction by Paul Smith

Obeyd Zakani is an important a figure in Persian and Sufi literature and poetry. His satire, humorous stories, ribald and obscene poems, social commentary, mystical *ghazals*, prose, *ruba'is* and his famous epic *qasida* 'Mouse & Cat' are popular today and are more relevant than ever. He is considered to be one of the world's greatest satirist and social-commentator whose life and mystical poems had a great influence on his student and friend Hafiz and many others. Here are most of his hilarious and often obscene satirical prose works, mostly fully translated... Including his *Definitions, Joyous Treatise, The Ethics of the Nobles, The Book of the Beard* and *A Hundred Maxims*. Included is a long Introduction on his Life & Times in Shiraz and his relationship to Hafiz and the princess poet, Jahan Khatun. Selected Bibliography. 212 pages

KHAQANI: SELECTED POEMS
Translation & Introduction by Paul Smith

Born in Shirwan in 1122 he died in Tabriz in 1199. He was a great poet and a master of the *qasida* and one of the first of the *ghazal*. He was born into the family of a carpenter in Melgem, near Shamakhy. He lost his father and was brought up by an uncle, a doctor and astronomer at court of the Shirwanshah, who acted 'as his nurse and tutor'. His mother was a Christian and Jesus features in many of his poems. After he was invited to court he assumed the pen-name Khaqani ('regal'). A court poet's life bored him and he fled to Iraq inspiring his famous *masnavi* 'A Gift from the Two Iraqs'. He also wrote 'The Ruin of Madain' painting his impression of the remains of Sassanid's Palace near the Ctesiphon. Returning home Shah Akhistan ordered his imprisonment. Released he moved to Tabriz but his small son died, then daughter, then wife. Alone, he soon died. He is buried at the Poet's Cemetery in Tabriz. He left a remarkable, large heritage of poems in Persian that influenced many 'court' and Sufi poets. A major influence on his poems was Sana'i. Introduction on his Life, Poetry & Times and Forms he composed in. The correct rhyme-structure has been kept in this largest selection of his poems including *ruba'is, ghazals, masnavi, qasidas, qit'as* in English. Selected Bibliography. 195 pages.

IBN 'ARABI: SELECTED POEMS
Translation & Introduction by Paul Smith

In the West he is known as the *Doctor Maximus* and in the Islamic world as *The Great Master*. Born in Murcia in Spain in 1165 his family moved to Seville. At thirty-five he left for Mecca where he completed his most influential book of poems *The Interpreter of Ardent Desires* and began writing his masterpiece, the vast *Meccan Revelations*. In 1204 he began further travels. In 1223 he settled in Damascus where he lived the last seventeen years of his life, being executed in 1240. His tomb there is still an important place of pilgrimage. A prolific writer, Ibn 'Arabi is generally known as the prime exponent of the idea later known as the 'Unity of Being'. His emphasis was on the true potential of the human being and the path to realizing that potential and becoming the Perfect or complete person. Hundreds of works are attributed to him including a large *Divan* of poems most of which have yet to be translated. Introduction on his life and poetry. The correct rhyme-structure has been kept as well as the beauty and meaning of this selection of his beautiful, mystical poems. 121 pages.

RIBALD POEMS OF THE SUFI POETS
Sana'i, Anvari, Mahsati, Rumi, Sadi, Obeyd Zakani
Translations, Introductions Paul Smith
Some of the greatest of the Persian Sufi poets composed ribald and at times 'obscene' poems for satirical and often (as in the case of Rumi) for teaching some spiritual truth or moral. Here is a wide-ranging selection of the greatest of them from the eleventh to the fourteenth century. Here are at times hilarious, witty, weird, and erotic and obscene poems in most of the various forms of classical Persian poetry... the *ghazal*, the *ruba'i*, the *masnavi*, the *qit'a*, the *qasida* and the *tarji-band*. 190 pages.

THE GHAZAL IN SUFI & DERVISH POETRY: An Anthology
Translations, Introductions, Etc. by Paul Smith
Introduction includes: The *Ghazal* in Arabic, Persian, Turkish, Urdu, Punjabi, Sindhi, Pushtu, Kashmiri & English Sufi & Dervish Poetry; Sufis & Dervishes: Their Art and Use of Poetry. Glossary of Sufi Symbols. Included with each selection of a poet is a brief biography plus a list of further reading. The correct rhyme-structure has been kept as well as the beauty and meaning of these beautiful, mystical poems.
THE POETS... Hazrat Ali page 33, Rabi'a of Basra 34, Dhu'l-Nun 38, Mansur al-Hallaj 40, Rudaki 42, Baba Kuhi 44, Sana'i 45, Khaqani 48, Nizami 50, 'Attar 54, Kamal ud-din 65, Ibn al-Farid 66, Ibn 'Arabi 69, Rumi 74, Imami 88, Sadi 69, Iraki 118, Humam 125, Yunus Emre 127, Amir Khusraw 138, Hasan Dihlavi 148, Auhadi 150, Ibn Yamin 152, Khaju 153, Obeyd Zakani 158, Emad 167, Hafiz 176, Ruh Attar 213, Ahmedi 218, Haydar 222, Junaid Shirazi 226, Kadi Burhan-ud-din 230, Jahan Khatun 233, Kamal 252, Maghribi 255, Nesimi 264, Sheykhi 273, Kasim Anwar 276, Shah Ni'matu'llah 280, Jami 281, Baba Fighani 293, Pir Sultan 298, Khayali 302, Fuzuli 308, Huda'i 317, Qutub Shah 325, Mirza 327, Sa'ib 337, Khushal 340, Ashraf Khan 349, Makhfi 354, Bedil 385, Abdul-Khadir 389, Rahman Baba 395, Khwaja Mohammad 409, Hamid 419, Niyazi 428, Wali 430, Mushtaq 434, Ali Haider 436, Sauda 437, Dard 439, Nazir 455, Mir 462, Sachal Sarmast 468, Galib 473, Esrar Dede 479, Aatish 481, Zauq 484, Tahirah 487, Shad 491, Iqbal 495, Ashgar 500, Jigar 503, Huma 508, Veysel 532, Paul 536. Pages 560.

MAKHFI: THE PRINCESS SUFI POET ZEB-UN-NISSA
A Selection of Poems from her *Divan*
Translation & Introduction by Paul Smith
Makhfi (1638-1702) pen-name meaning 'concealed', was Zeb-un-Nissa the beautiful and talented oldest daughter of the strict Muslim Emperor of

India, Aurangzeb. She was imprisoned for 20 years for her Sufi views and conspiring with a brother against him. Her over 550 *ghazals* and *ruba'is* in Persian are deep, spiritual and at times truly heartbreaking.
The correct forms and spiritual meaning are preserved in this large selection of her poetry. Selected Bibliography. 126 pages.

~THE SUFI RUBA'IYAT~A Treasury of Sufi and Dervish Poetry in the Ruba'i form, from Rudaki to the 21st Century
Translations, Introductions, Notes etc. by Paul Smith
Introduction includes...Sufis & Dervishes: Their Art and Use of Poetry... The Form of the Ruba'i in Persian, Arabic, Turkish, Urdu & English Sufi & Dervish Poetry & a Glossary. Included with each selection of a particular poet is a brief biography plus a list of further reading. The correct rhyme-structure has been kept as well as the beauty and meaning of these beautiful, mystical poems. THE POETS...Rudaki page 31, Mansur al-Hallaj 34, Shibli 36, Baba Tahir 37, Abu Said 42, Ibn Sina 48, Baba Kuhi 51, Ansari 52, Al-Ghazzali 54, Hamadani 56, Sana'i 58, Mahsati 62, Khaqani 66, Nizami 70, Ruzbihan 72, Baghdadi 74, 'Attar 76, Auhad-ud-din Kermani 83, Kamal ud-din 87, Hamavi 91, Baba Afzal 93, Rumi 96, Imami 106, Sadi 107, Iraki 112, Sultan Valad 117, Humam 119, Amir Khusraw 121, Simnani 125, Ibn Yamin 127, Khaju 128, Obeyd Zakani 130, Emad 132, Hafiz 133, Ruh Attar 141, Kadi Burhan-ud-din 142, Jahan Khatun 144, Kamal 152, Maghribi 152, Nesimi 155, Kasim Anwar 158, Shah Ni'matu'llah 159, Jami 162, Baba Fighani 165, Fuzuli 166, Ghazali 168, Urfi 170, Qutub Shah 172, Haleti 174, Dara Shikoh 176, Sarmad 179, Sa'ib 189, Nasir Ali 190, Makhfi 191, Bedil 194, Mushtaq 188, Sauda 200, Dard 203, Esrar Dede 205, Hatif 206, Mir 208, Aatish 211, Zauq 213, Dabir 215, Anees 216, Hali 218, Shad 220, Iqbal 222, Khalili 225, Rahi 229, Nurbakhsh, Paul 232. Pages... 244.

RUBAI'YAT OF THE WORLD: An Anthology
Court, Sufi, Dervish, Satirical, Ribald, Prison and Social Poetry in the Ruba'i form from the 9th to the 20th century from the Arabic, Persian, Turkish and Urdu
Translations, Introduction and Notes by Paul Smith
Introduction includes chapter on the ruba'i. Included with each selection of a particular poet is a brief biography plus a list of further reading. The correct rhyme-structure has been kept as well as the beauty and meaning of these beautiful, often mystical poems.
THE POETS... Hanzalah page 11, Mansur-al Hallaj 12, Shibli 15, Abu Shakur 16, Shahid 17, Rudaki 18, Rabi'a Balkhi 122, Daqiqi 24, Umarah 27, Firdausi 28, Baba Tahir 31, Farrukhi 36, Asjadi 38, Unsuri 39, Abu Said 42,

Ibn Sina 49, Baba Kuhi 52, Azraqi 54, Qatran 56, Ansari 58, Al-Ghazali 61, Mas'ud Sad 63, Mu'izzi 68, Hamadani 71, Omar Khayyam 74, Sana'i 77, Sabir 82, Mahsati 83, Jabali 93, Vatvat 95, Anvari 98, Khaqani 103, Zahir 108, Nizami 111, Ruzbihan 113, Baghdadi 115, 'Attar 118, Auhad ud-din Kermani 126, Kamal ad-din 132, Hamavi 136, Baba Afzal 139, Rumi 142, Imami 153, Hamgar 154, Sadi 158, Iraki 165, Sultan Valad 161, Humam 173, Amir Khusraw 176, Simnani 180, Ibn Yamin 183, Khaju 185, Obeyd Zakani 188, Emad 193, Salman 195, Hafiz 197, Ruh Attar 206, Kadi Burhan-ud-din 208, Jahan Khatun 210, Shah Shuja 220, Kamal 223, Maghribi 224, Bushaq 227, Kasim Anwar 232, Shah Ni'tmu'llah 234, Nesimi 237, Jami 241, Nejati 244, Baba Fighani 246, Babur 248, Humayan 251, Kamran 254, Fuzuli 256, Ghazali 254, Kahi 257, Akbar 258, Urfi 260, Hayati 263, Ulfati 264, Qutub Shah 269, Haleti 271, Dara Shikoh 274, Sarmad 277, Sa'ib 285, Nasir Ali 287, Makhfi 289, Nabi 292, Bedil 294, Nedim 300, Mushtaq 302, Sauda 305. Dard 308, Esrar Dede 311, Nishat 313, Hatif 315, Mir 317, Aatish 321, Zauq 323, Ghalib 325, Momin 329, Dabir 332, Anees 334, Hali 337, Akbar Allahbadi 339, Shad 341, Iqbal 343, Mehroom 347, Firaq 349, Josh 352, Khalili 357, Rahi 361, Faiz, Nurbaksh 364. Pages 367.

LOVE'S AGONY & BLISS: ANTHOLOGY OF URDU POETRY
Sufi, Dervish, Court and Social Poetry from the 16th-20th Century
Translations, Introductions, Etc. by Paul Smith

Introduction includes…The Urdu Language, Urdu Poetry, The Ghazal in Urdu Poetry, Ghazal Singing in India & Pakistan, The Ruba'i in Urdu Poetry, The Masnavi in Urdu Poetry, Glossary for Sufi & Dervish Urdu Poetry. Included with each selection of a particular poet is a brief biography plus a list of further reading. The correct rhyme-structure has been kept as well as the beauty and meaning of these beautiful, often mystical poems. THE POETS…Qutub Shah page 29, Wali 34, Sauda 43, Dard 51, Nazir 60, Mir 74, Aatish 96, Zauq 107, Ghalib 114, Momin 130, Dabir 138, Anees 142, Hali 146, Akbar Allahabadi 150, Shad 152, Iqbal 160, Asghar 170, Mehroom 175, Josh 177, Jigar 187, Huma 196, Firaq 216, Faiz 228. Pages 230.

BREEZES OF TRUTH
Selected Early & Classical Arabic Sufi Poetry
Translations, Introductions, Etc., by Paul Smith

Introduction includes…Sufis: Their Art and Use of Poetry & The Main Forms in Arabic Sufi Poetry.
Included with each selection of a particular poet is a brief biography plus a list of further reading. The correct rhyme-structure has been kept as well as the beauty and meaning of these beautiful, mystical poems.

THE POETS... Hazrat Ali page 19, Ali Ibn Husain 21, Rabi'a of Basra 23, Dhu'l-Nun 36, Bayazid Bistami 47, Al Nuri 50, Junaid 44, Sumnun 65, Mansur al-Hallaj 71, Shibli 101, Ibn Sina 111, Al-Ghazzali 114, Gilani 118, Suhrawadi 122, Ibn al-Farid 129, Ibn 'Arabi 143. Pages 185.

THE~DIVINE~WINE : A Treasury of Sufi and Dervish Poetry
(Volume One)
Translations, Introductions, Etc. by Paul Smith
Introduction includes...Sufis & Dervishes: Their Art and Use of Poetry, The Main Forms in Arabic, Persian, Turkish, Kashmiri, Hindi, Urdu, Punjabi, Sindhi & English Sufi & Dervish Poetry. Glossary of Sufi & Dervish Symbols. Included with each selection of a particular poet is a brief biography plus a list of further reading. The correct rhyme-structure has been kept as well as the beauty and meaning of these beautiful, mystical poems.
THE POETS... Hazrat Ali page 39, Ali Ibn Husain 40, Rabi'a of Basra 40, Dhu'l-Nun 46, Bayazid Bistami 53, Al Nuri 54, Junaid 57, Sumnun 59, Mansur al-Hallaj 60, Rudaki 67, Shibli 72, Baba Tahir 74, Abu Said 78, Ibn Sina 85, Baba Kuhi 88, Ansari 90, Al-Ghazzali 92, Hamadani 95, Sana'i 98, Gilani 109, Mahsati 112, Khaqani 117, Suhrawadi 122, Nizami 126, Ruzbihan 150, Baghdadi 152, 'Attar 154, Auhad-ud-din Kermani 177, Kamal ud-din 182, Ibn al-Farid 186, Ibn 'Arabi 197, Baba Farid 206, Hamavi 213, Baba Afzal 216, Rumi 218, Imami 269, Sadi 271, Iraki 341, Sultan Valad 352, Humam 358, Yunus Emre 362, Amir Khusraw 375, Hasan Dihlavi 386, Simnani 388, Auhadi 391, Ibn Yamin 395, Khaju 398, Obeyd Zakani 404, Emad 417, Lalla Ded 426, Hafiz 429, Jahan Khatun 490. Pages 550.

THE~DIVINE~WINE: A Treasury of Sufi and Dervish Poetry
(Volume Two)
Translations, Introductions, Etc. by Paul Smith
Introduction includes...Sufis & Dervishes: Their Art and Use of Poetry... The Main Forms in Arabic, Persian, Turkish, Kashmiri, Hindi, Urdu, Punjabi, Pusthu, Sindhi & English Sufi & Dervish Poetry. Glossary of Sufi Symbols. The correct rhyme-structure has been kept as well as the beauty and meaning of these beautiful, mystical poems.
Included with each poet is a brief biography plus a list of further reading.
THE POETS: Ruh Attar page 39, Haydar 47, Junaid Shirazi 58, Ahmedi 62, Kadi Burhan-ud-din 66, Kamal 70, Maghribi 74, Nesimi 83, Sheykhi 95, Kasim Anwar 97, Shah Ni'matu'llah 104, Kabir 110, Jami 125, Fighani 141, Pir Sultan 147, Khayali 150, Fuzuli 156, Huda'i 167, Urfi 169, Qutub Shah 173, Mirza 176, Nef'i 190, Sa'ib 197, Dara Shikoh 200, Sarmad 202, Khushal

212, Sultan Bahu 221, Ashraf Khan 226, Nasir Ali 231, Makhfi 232, Bedil 265, Abdul-Khan 273, Rahman Baba 279, Khwaja Mohammad 296, Hamid 305, Niyazi 316, Wali 319, Bulleh Shah 323, Shah Latif 329, Mushtaq 337, Ali Haider 341, Sauda 343, Dard 347, Ahmad Shah 351, Shaida 358, Nazir 364, Hatif 377, Mir 384, Sachal Sarmast 395, Galib 400, Esrar Dede 406, Aatish 409, Zauq 413, Dabir 416, Anees 418, Tahirah 420, Hali 429, Farid 431, Shad 433, Iqbal 438, Inayat Khan 448, Ashgar 463, Jigar 465, Huma 470, Veysel 498, Firaq 501, Josh 506, Brabazon 510, Khalili 518, Nurbaksh 522, Paul 524. Pages 556.

TONGUES ON FIRE: An Anthology of the Sufi, Dervish, Warrior & Court Poetry of Afghanistan.
Translations, Introductions, Etc. by Paul Smith
Introduction includes… The Main Forms in Dari/Persian, and Pushtu Poetry; Sufis & Dervishes: Their Art and Use of Poetry. Glossary. Included with each selection of a particular poet is a brief biography plus a list of further reading. The correct rhyme-structure has been kept as well as the beauty and meaning of these beautiful and mainly mystical poems.
THE POETS… Hanzalah page 19, Abu Shakur 21, Shahid 24, Rudaki 27, Rabai'a Balkhi 38, Daqiqi 47, Nasir-i-Khusraw 55, Ansari 59, Azraqi 63, Sana'i 66, Zahir 81, Rumi 96, Imami 151, Jami 155, Mirza 176, Khushal 194, Ashraf Khan 212, Bedil 219, Abdul-Kadir 229, Rahman Baba 237, Khwaja Mohammad 257, Hamid 270, Ahmad Shah 287, Shaida 297, Khalili 303. 325 pages.

THE SEVEN GOLDEN ODES (QASIDAS) OF ARABIA
(The *Mu'allaqat*)
Translations, Introduction & Notes by Paul Smith
The *Mu'allaqat* is the title of a group of seven long Arabic odes or *qasidas* that have come down from the time before Islam. Each is considered the best work of these pre-Islamic poets. The name means 'The Suspended *Qasidas*' or 'The Hanging Poems', the traditional explanation being that these poems were hung on or in the Kaaba at Mecca.
These famous ancient Arabic *qasidas* are formed of three parts: they start, with a nostalgic opening in which the poet reflects on what has passed, known as *nasib*. A common concept is the pursuit of the poet of the caravan of his love; by the time he reaches their campsite they have already moved on. The second section is *rahil* (travel section) in which the poet contemplates the harshness of nature and life away from the tribe. Finally there is the message of the poem, which can take several forms: praise of the tribe, *fakhr*; satire about other tribes, *hija*; or some moral maxims, *hikam*.

Included with each qasida of each poet is a brief biography plus a list of further reading. The correct rhyme-structure has been kept as well as the beauty and meaning of these beautiful poems.
CONTENTS: The Introduction... The *Mu'allaqat* 7, The *Qasida* 17. The Poets... Imra'ul-Qays 19, Tarafa 37, Amru 59, Harith 73, Antara 83, Zuhair 103, Labid 119. Appendix... Kab's *Qasida* of the Mantle 139. Pages... 140.

THE QASIDA: A WORLD ANTHOLOGY
Translations, Introduction & Notes by Paul Smith
The *qasida* is a form of praise poetry from pre-Islamic Arabia. It sometimes runs to more than 50 lines and sometimes more than 100. It was later inherited by the Persians, the Turks, the Afghans and Urdu Poets where it was developed immensely by Sufi, court and tribal poets. The *qasida* resembles a *ghazal* in many ways except that it is longer. In the first couplet, both the lines rhyme, and the same rhyme runs through the whole poem, the rhyme-word being at the end of the second line of each couplet (after the first couplet).
Included with each selection of a particular poet is a brief biography plus a list of further reading. The correct rhyme-structure has been kept as well as the beauty and meaning of these beautiful poems.
CONTENTS: Introduction: The *Qasida:* The Beginnings in Arabia... The Persian *Qasida*... *Qasida* in Turkey.
THE POETS (In Order of Appearance) Imra' ul-Qays 13, Tarafa 25, Amru 39, Harith 48, Antara 55, Zuhair 68, Labid 78, Ka'b 90, Rudaki 28, Dhu'l-Nun 99, Kisa'i 104, Farrukhi 106, Minuchirhri 114, Unsuri 119, Ibn Sina 123, Nasir-i-Khusraw 125, Al-Ghazali 128, Asadi 131, Azraqi 137, Qatran 139, Mas'ud Sad 143, Mu'izzi 149, Sana'i 154, Jabali 159, Gilani 162, Anvari 165, Falaki 169, Khaqani 172, Abu Madyan 178, Suhrawardi 183, Zahir 187, Nizami 193, Ibn al-Farid 197, Ibn 'Arabi 209, Hamgar 213, Iraki 215, Humam 218, Amir Khusraw 220, Auhadi 224, Obeyd Zakani 226, Salman 234, Hafiz 239, Ruh Attar 255, Haydar 259, Azad 267, Shah Shuja 269, Shah Ni'tmu'llah 272, Necati 276, Fuzuli 282, Baqi 285, Urfi 290, Mirza 292, Nef'i 298, Niyazi 301, Khushal 304, Rahman Baba 310, Hamid 314, Ghalib 317, Parvin 322, Paul 328.   407 pages.

IBN AL-FARID: WINE & THE MYSTIC'S PROGRESS
Translation, Introduction & Notes by Paul Smith
Umar Ibn al-Farid, an Egyptian poet (1181-1235), is considered to be the undisputed master of Islamic mystical poetry into Arabic. He is considered not only to be a poet but a Perfect Master *(Qutub)* a God-realised soul...

and it is his journey to unity with God that he reveals in probably the
longest *qasida* (ode) in Arabic (761 couplets), his famous *The Mystic's
Progress*. The other poem for which he is most known is his *Wine Poem*
that is often seen as a prologue to the *The Mystic's Progress*.
Although these long poems have been translated into English before this is
the first time in the correct rhyme of the *qasida* and in clear, concise, modern
English. Included in the Introduction are chapters on his Life & Work, The
Qasida in Arabic, Previous *Qasidas* by Master Arab Poets that would
have influenced him, The Perfect Master *(Qutub)*, and the *Wine Poem and
The Mystic's Way*. Selected Bibliography. The correct rhyme-structure has
been kept as well as the beauty and meaning of these beautiful poems.
Appendix upon the other translations into English of both poems. 174 pages.

RUBA'IYAT OF ABU SA'ID
Translation, Introduction & Notes by Paul Smith.
Abu Sa'id ibn Abi 'l-Khair (968-1049) was a Perfect Master and a poet who
lived in Nishapur and composed only *ruba'is*, over 400 of them. He was a
founder of Sufi poetry and a major influence on the *ruba'i* and most poets
that followed, especially Sana'i, Nizami, 'Attar, Rumi and Hafiz. Here are
188 of his poems translated into the correct form. Included in the
Introduction is the life of Abu Sa'id and a history of the *ruba'i* and examples
by its greatest exponents. Selected Bibliography. The correct rhyme-
structure is kept as well as the beauty and meaning of these immortal four-
line poems. 227 pages.

RUBA'IYAT OF BABA TAHIR
Translations, Introduction & Notes by Paul Smith
Baba Tahir, or Oryan ('The Naked') of Hamadan... approx. 990-1065, was
a great God-intoxicated, or God-mad soul *(mast)* and possibly a *Qutub*
(Perfect Master) who composed about 120 known *ruba'i* in a simpler metre
than the usual *'hazaj'* metre. His simple, mystical poems that he would sing
while wandering naked throughout the land had a profound influence on
Sufis and dervishes and other *ruba'i* composers, especially Abu Sa'id, Ibn
Sina and Omar Khayyam. Included in the Introduction is the life of Baba
Tahir and a history of the *ruba'i* and examples by its greatest exponents.
Selected Bibliography. The correct rhyme-structure has been kept as well as
the beauty and meaning of these immortal four-line poems. 154 pages.

THE POETS OF SHIRAZ
Sufi, Dervish, Court & Satirical Poets from the 9th to the 20th Centuries
of the fabled city of Shiraz

Translations & Introduction & Notes by Paul Smith
CONTENTS: Shiraz in History. The Various Forms in Classical Persian Poetry, Sufism in Persian Poetry, A Glossary of Sufi & Dervish Poetry
THE POETS OF SHIRAZ… 49 Mansur al-Hallaj 51, Baba Kuhi 59, Ruzbihan 59, Hamgar 65, Sadi 70, Nasir 123, Khaju 127, Obeyd Zakani 136, Emad 187, Shahin 199, Hafiz 218, Ruh Attar 299, Haydar 313, Yazdi 326, Azad 328, Junaid 332, Jalal 336, Jahan Khatun 337, Shah Shuja 381, Bushaq 387, Shah Da'i, 400, Ahli 407, Figani 409, Urfi 414, Visal 419, Qa'ani 420, Shurida 427, Munis 'Ali Shah 429, Lotfali Suratgar 433, Mehdi Hamidi 436. 436 pages.

RUBA'IYAT OF 'ATTAR
Translation, Introduction & Notes by Paul Smith
Farid ad-din 'Attar (d. 1221) is the Perfect Master Poet who was the author of over forty books of poetry and prose including *The Conference of the Birds, The Book of God* (which he is said to have presented to Rumi when he met him) and *The Lives of the Saints*. Apart from his many books in *masnavi* form he also composed many hundreds of mystical *ghazals* and *ruba'is*. He also changed the evolution of the *ruba'i* form by composing a long Sufi epic, the *Mukhtar-nama*, where each of 2088 *ruba'is* is connected by subject matter that Fitzgerald attempted to do with those he attributed to Omar Khayyam.
Included in the Introduction is the life of 'Attar and a history of the *ruba'i* and examples by its greatest exponents. Selected Bibliography. The correct rhyme-structure has been kept as well as the beauty and meaning of these immortal four-line poems. 114 Pages.

RUBA'IYAT OF MAHSATI
Translation, Introduction & Notes by Paul Smith
We know little of Mahsati Ganjavi's life (1098-1185) except that she lived in Ganjeh where Sultan Sanjar reigned and as she was a poet at his court she would have known Anvari. She was a court, dervish and ribald poet. She knew Nizami (she is said to have been buried in his mausoleum) and Omar Khayyam… and like Omar composed only in the *ruba'i* form and must be considered not only a master of that form but also to have helped revolutionize it. She was an influence on perhaps Iran's greatest female poet Jahan Khatun of Shiraz and Iran's greatest satirist Obeyd Zakani. She was famous and also infamous for her liberated behaviour. Included in the Introduction are the life of Mahsati and a history of the *ruba'i* and examples by its greatest exponents. Selected Bibliography. The correct rhyme-

structure has been kept as well as the beauty and meaning of these immortal four-line poems. 144 Pages.

RUBA'IYAT OF JAHAN KHATUN
Translation by Paul Smith & Rezvaneh Pashai
Introduction & Notes by Paul Smith
Jahan Khatun (1326-1416?) was the daughter of the king of one of Shiraz's most turbulent times... Masud Shah; pupil and lifelong friend of the world's greatest mystical, lyric poet, Hafiz of Shiraz; the object of crazed desire by (among others) Iran's greatest satirist, the obscene, outrageous, visionary poet Obeyd Zakani; lover, then wife of womanizer Amin al-Din, a minister of one of Persia's most loved, debauched and tragic rulers... Abu Ishak. She was cruelly imprisoned for twenty years under the Muzaffarids while her young daughter mysteriously died; open-minded and scandalous, one of Iran's first feminists... the beautiful and sensuous, petite princess who abdicated her royalty twice is one of Iran's greatest classical lyric poets whose *Divan* is four times larger than that of Hafiz's and contains about 2000 *ghazals* and many hundreds of wonderful *ruba'is*. Included in the Introduction is the life of Jahan and a history of the *ruba'i* and examples by its greatest exponents. Selected Bibliography. The correct rhyme-structure has been kept as well as the beauty and meaning of these immortal four-line poems. 157 Pages.

RUBA'IYAT OF SANA'I
Translation, Introduction & Notes by Paul Smith
One of the most prolific and influential Sufi Master Poets of all time Hakim Sana'i (d.1131) composed many *ghazals, masnavis* and over 400 *ruba'is* that influenced all the *ruba'i* writers that followed him, especially Mahsati and 'Attar. His long *masnavi* (rhyming couplets) mystical work *The Enclosed Garden of the Truth* is said to have had a profound influence on Rumi's composing of his *Masnavi* and in Sadi's composing his *Bustan* ('The Orchard'). Included in the Introduction are the life of Sana'i and a history of the *ruba'i* and examples by its greatest exponents. Selected Bibliography. The correct rhyme-structure has been kept as well as the beauty and meaning of these immortal four-line poems. 111 Pages.

RUBA'IYAT OF JAMI
Translation, Introduction & Notes by Paul Smith
Jami (1414-1493), considered the last great poet of the Classical Period (10th-15thC.) is mostly known for his masterpiece seven *masnavis* epics... including *Joseph and Zulaikh, Layla and Majnun,* and *Salman and Absal.*

He also composed three *Divans* consisting of *ghazals rubai's* and other profound mystical poems. Here are 103 *ruba'is,* the largest number ever put into English. Included in the Introduction are the life of Jami and a history of the *ruba'i* and examples by its greatest exponents. Selected Bibliography. The correct rhyme-structure has been kept as well as the beauty and meaning of these beautiful, mystical four-line poems. 178 Pages.

RUBA'IYAT OF SARMAD
Translation, Introduction & Notes by Paul Smith
Sarmad (d. 1659) or Hazrat Sarmad Shaheed, whose name 'Sarmad' derives from the Persian word for eternal or everlasting, was a famous and infamous Persian dervish poet of Jewish and Armenian origin. As a merchant he gathered his wares and travelled to India to sell them. In India he renounced Judaism and adopted Islam: he later renounced it in favour of Hinduism which he finally renounced for Sufism. He was known for exposing and ridiculing the major religions and hypocrisy of his day, but he also wrote beautiful mystical poetry in the form of 321 *rubai's* (all here translated). He wandered the streets and the courts of the emperor as a naked dervish. He was beheaded in 1659 by Emperor Aurangzeb for his perceived heretical poetry. His grave is located near the Jama Masjid in Delhi. 381 pages.

RUBA'IYAT OF HAFIZ
Translation, Introduction & Notes by Paul Smith
Persia's greatest exponent of the *ghazal* Hafiz (1320-1392) became a Perfect Master *(Qutub),* was twice exiled from his beloved Shiraz for his criticism of rulers and false Sufi masters and hypocritical clergy. His *Divan* shows he composed in other forms including the *ruba'i* of which about 160 survive. As with his *ghazals,* his *ruba'is* are sometimes mystical and sometimes critical of the hypocrisy of his times. Included in the Introduction is the life of Hafiz and a history of the *ruba'i* and examples by its greatest exponents. Selected Bibliography. The correct rhyme-structure has been kept as well as the beauty and meaning of these immortal four-line poems. 220 Pages.

YUNUS EMRE, THE TURKISH DERVISH: SELECTED POEMS
Translation, Introduction & Notes by Paul Smith
Yunus Emre (d. 1320) is considered one of the most important Turkish poets having a great influence on Turkish literature from his own time until today. His poems concern divine love as well as human love of the Divine as God and the Perfect Master, Beloved, Friend and human destiny and weakness. Little is known of his life other than he became a Sufi dervish Perfect Master *(Qutub).* A contemporary of Rumi, it is told the two great souls

met: Rumi asked Yunus what he thought of his huge work, the *Mesnevi*. Yunus said, "Excellent! But I would have done it differently." Surprised, Rumi asked how. Yunus replied, "I'd have written, 'I came from the eternal, clothed myself in flesh, took the name Yunus.'" This illustrates his simple approach that has made him loved by many. His poems were probably a great influence on Hafiz who was born the year he died and who knew Turkish. Here is the largest selection of his poems translated into English mainly in the form of the *gazel* that he often used. The correct rhyme-structure has been kept as well as the beauty and meaning of these beautiful, mystical poems.

Included… an Introduction on his Life & Times and the Form and History & Function of the *gazel* and a chapter on Sufism & Poetry, Turkish Poetry and the Turkish Language and a Selected Bibliography. Pages… 237

RUBA'IYAT OF KAMAL AD-DIN
Translation, Introduction & Notes by Paul Smith

Kamal ad-din Isma'il (1172-1238) known as 'The Creator of Subtle Thoughts' was the son of the court poet Jamal ad-din and was one of the last of the great poets of the early days in Isfahan. Both father and son praised their city and the same patrons but Kamal ad-din considered himself not only a court poet but a Sufi or Dervish. His *qasidas* in the style of Iraki were greatly admired and some were said to 'reach the summit of perfection' but it is his many much loved human and divine *ruba'is* that his fame now rests upon. Here are the largest number of his *ruba'is* ever put into English. Included in the Introduction… the Life and Times of Kamal ad-din and a history of the *ruba'i* and examples by its greatest exponents and a chapter on Sufi Poetry. The correct rhyme-structure has been kept and the beauty and meaning of these beautiful, mystical, loving, sometimes satirical four-line poems. Pages 152.

RUBA'YAT OF KHAYYAM
Translation, Introduction & Notes by Paul Smith
Reprint of 1909 Introduction by R.A. Nicholson

Of the 900 to 2000 or so *ruba'is* attributed to Omar Khayyam (died 1132) over 500 years only about ten to twenty percent are now considered to be his. More famous in Iran as an astronomer and mathematician… his nihilistic and hedonistic and occasionally Sufi philosophy in his *ruba'is* meant that his poems were never really popular in his homeland, but of course after the work of FitzGerald the west fell in love with him. Included in the Introduction… the Life and Times of Omar Khayyam and his work as a Scientist & Philosopher and a history of the *ruba'i* and examples by its greatest exponents and a chapter on the various translations into English and other languages. Selected bibliography. The correct rhyme-structure has been kept as well as the beauty and meaning of these beautiful, fatalistic, intoxicated, loving, sometimes mystical and satirical 186 four-line poems. 266 pages.

RUBA'IYAT OF AUHAD UD-DIN
Translation and Introduction by Paul Smith

Auhad ud-din Kermani (1164-1238) was influenced by 'Attar, Ibn 'Arabi (whom he knew) and Suhrawadi and was a powerful speaker and a Sufi Master whose disciples at one time numbered over 70,000.
He used the *ruba'i* form (composing over 1700) in his teaching although he also composed in other forms. Among his followers was Auhadi of Maragha who took his *takhallus* or pen-name from his master. His ideas and behaviour was said to have shocked many of his fellow Sufis and contemporaries. Included in the Introduction... the Life and Work of Auhad ud-din and a history of the *ruba'i* and examples by its greatest exponents and a chapter on Sufi Poetry. The correct rhyme-structure has been kept as well as the beauty and meaning of these mystical, loving four-line poems. 109 pages.

HUMA: SELECTED POEMS OF MEHER BABA
Translation & Introduction by Paul Smith

Merwan S. Irani (1894-1969), known world-wide as Meher Baba, took Huma (Phoenix) as his *takhallus* or pen-name when he composed enlightened *ghazals* in a mixture of Persian, Urdu and Gujarati in his twenties as a realized disciple of the *Qutub* or Perfect Master Upasni Maharaj, and also later on. He knew the *ghazals* of Hafiz by heart as did his father, the dervish Sheriar Irani, who had originally walked to Pune in India from Khooramshah in Iran. Merwan went on to reveal himself as *Qutub* and later also declared himself as the *Rasool* or Messiah (Avatar). The correct rhyme-structure has been kept as well as the beauty and meaning of these beautiful, mystical poems. Contents: The Life of Meher Baba... page 7, The *Ghazal,* its Form and History 21, Selected Bibliography 27 Ghazals 29, Qit'as (Fragments), 83. Ruba'is. Pages... 116.

RUBA'IYAT OF AL-MA'ARRI
Translation & Introduction by Paul Smith

CONTENTS: The Life and Works of al Ma'arri... Page 7 Selected Bibliography... 14, The *Ruba'i:* Its Form, Use and History... 15, Ruba'iyat of al-Ma'arri... 31.

Abu'l-'Ala al-Ma'arri was born in Ma'arra, south of Aleppo in Syria in 973 A.D. He achieved fame as one of greatest of Arab poets. Al-Ma'arri was stricken with smallpox when four and became blind. His early poems in *ruba'i* form gained great popularity. As he grew older, he was able to travel to Aleppo, Antioch and other Syrian cities. Al-Ma'arri spent 18 months at Baghdad, then the centre of learning and poetry, leaving to return to his native town. There he created the *Luzumiyyat*, a famous collection of 1592 poems. On return, his presence in al-Ma'arra drew many people, who came to hear him lecture on poetry and rhetoric. 128 pages.

ANTHOLOGY OF CLASSICAL ARABIC POETRY (From Pre-Islamic Times to Ibn 'Arabi)
Translations, Introduction and Notes by Paul Smith
CONTENTS: Classical Arabic Poetry... page 7, The Qasida... 10, The Qit'a... 11, The Ghazal... 12, The Ruba'i... 16, Selected Bibliography... 17: THE POETS (In Order of Appearance) Imra' ul-Qays 19, Zuhair 31, Harith 41, Antara 48, Tarafa 62, Amru 76, Al-A'sha 86, Suhaym 88, Labid 90, Ka'b 102, Khansa 107, Hazrat Ali 109, Ali Ibn Husain 111, Omar Ibn Abi Rabi'a 113, Majnun 116, Rab'ia of Basra 123, Bashshar 130, Abu Nuwas 133, Abu Tammam 153, Dhu'l-Nun 157, Bayazid Bistami 165, Al-Nuri 167, Junaid 171, Sumnun 173, Mansur al-Hallaj 175, Al-Mutanabbi 184, Al-Ma'arri 212, Ibn Sina 230, Al-Ghazali 233, Gilani 236, Abu Madyan 240, Suhrawardi 245, Ibn al-Farid 249, Ibn 'Arabi 262. Pages 272.

THE QIT'A: Anthology of the 'Fragment' in Arabic, Persian and Eastern Poetry.
Translations, Introduction and Notes by Paul Smith
Contents: Arabic Poetry... page 7, Persian Poetry... 10 The Form & Function of the Qit'a... 12 .THE POETS (In Order of Appearance) Al-A'sha 15, Khansa 17, Omar Ibn Abi Rabi'a 19, Suhaym 22, Ali Ibn Husain 24, Raba'i of Basra 26, Majnun 32, Bashshar 40, Abu Nuwas 43, Abu Tammam 63, Abbas of Merv 67, Hanzalah 69, Firuz 71, Dhu'l-Nun 73, Bayazid Bistami 76, Al-Nuri 78, Junaid 82, Sumnun 84, Mansur al-Hallaj 86, Abu Salik 93, Abu Shakur 95, Shibli 97, Junaidi 100, Shahid, 102, Rudaki 104, Agachi 108, Rabi'a Balkhi 110, Khusravani 113, Al-Mutanabbi 115, Manjik 118, Daqiqi 120, Mantiki 125, Umarah 127, Kisa'i 129, Firdausi 131, Farrukhi 134, Asjadi 136, Manuchihri 138, Unsuri 140, Al-Ma'arri 143, Azraqi 155, Mas'ud Sa'd 157, Suhrawardi 160, Al-Ghazali 163, Mu'izzi 166, Hamadani 169, Sana'i 171, Sabir 173, Mahsati 176, Jabali 179, Vatvat 181, Anvari 183, Falaki 198, Khaqani 202, Zahir 207, Ibn 'Arabi 210, Sadi 217, Amir Khusraw 220, Auhadi 223, Ibn Yamin 225, Obeyd Zakani 230, Salman

235, Hafiz 237, Ruh Attar 254, Junaid Shirazi 256, Jahan Khatun 259, Shah Shuja 266, Kasin Anwar 268, Jami 271, Helali, 274, Nef'i 276, Bedil 279, Ali Haidar 282, Mir 285, Qa'ani 288, Parvin 290, Huma 294. Pages 296.

HEARTS WITH WINGS Anthology of Persian Sufi and Dervish Poetry
Translations, Introductions, Etc., by Paul Smith
CONTENTS: Introduction...Persian Poetry: A New Beginning... Sufis & Dervishes: Their Art and Use of Poetry... The Main Forms in Persian Sufi & Dervish Poetry... Glossary. Included with each selection of a particular poet is a brief biography plus a list of further reading. The correct rhyme-structure has been kept as well as the beauty and meaning of these beautiful, mystical poems. THE POETS... Rudaki 41, Baba Tahir 46, Abu Said 50, Ibn Sina 57, Baba Kuhi 59, Ansari 61, Al-Ghazzali 63, Hamadani 66, Sana'i 69, Mahsati 81, Khaqani 86, Nizami 92, Ruzbihan 117, Baghdadi 119, 'Attar 121, Auhad-ud-din Kermani 144, Kamal ud-din 149, Hamavi 153, Baba Afzal 156, Rumi 159, Imami 210, Sadi 212, Iraki 282, Sultan Valad 284, Humam 286, Amir Khusraw 290, Hasan Dihlavi 302, Simnani 304, Auhadi 307, Ibn Yamin 312, Khaju 315, Obeyd Zakani 324, Emad 334, Hafiz 344, Jahan Khatun 405, Ruh Attar 436, Haydar 444, Junaid Shirazi 356, Kamal 460, Maghribi 464, Kasim Anwar 474, Shah Ni'matu'llah 482, Jami 489, Fighani 506, Urfi 511, Sa'ib 515, Dara Shikoh 518, Sarmad 529, Nasir Ali 531, Makhfi 533, Bedil 567, Mushtaq 575, Hatif 579, Tahirah 586, Iqbal 595, Khalili 603, Nurbaksh 607. Pages 660

HAFIZ: SELECTED POEMS
Translation, Introduction & Notes by Paul Smith
Persia's greatest exponent of the *ghazal* Hafiz (1320-1390) became a Perfect Master *(Qutub)*, was twice exiled from his beloved Shiraz for his criticism of rulers and false Sufi masters and hypocritical clergy. His *Divan* shows he composed in nearly all forms. As with his *ghazals,* his *masnavis, qasidas, qita's, ruba'is* and other poems are sometimes mystical and sometimes critical of the hypocrisy of his times. Included in the Introduction is the Life and Times and Poetry of Hafiz and a history of the various forms. Selected Bibliography. Glossary. The correct rhyme-structure has been kept as well as the beauty and meaning of these immortal four-line poems. 227 Pages.

'ATTAR: SELECTED POETRY
Translation, Introduction & Notes by Paul Smith
Farid ad-din 'Attar is seen with Sana'i and Rumi (who he met and influenced) as one of the three most important Sufi Poet –Masters of the 13th century. He composed over forty books mainly in the epic *masnavi* form

of rhyming couplets, his most famous being *The Book of God* and *The Conference of the Birds*. He also composed many powerful mystical poems in the *ghazal* form and in the *ruba'i* form. Here for the first time is a fine selection of his poems in all three forms in the correct-rhyme structure with the beauty and meaning of his immortal poems. Introduction on his Life & Times and Poetry and an essay by Inayat Khan on Sufi Poetry. Selected Bibliography & Glossary. 177 pages.

SANA'I : SELECTED POEMS
Translation, Introduction & Notes by Paul Smith
One of the most prolific and influential Sufi Master Poets of all time Hakim Sana'i (d.1131) composed many *ghazals, masnavis, qasidas, qita's* and over 400 *ruba'is* that influenced all the *ruba'i* writers that followed him. His long *masnavi* (rhyming couplets) mystical work *The Enclosed Garden of the Truth* is said to have had a profound influence on Rumi's composing of his *Masnavi* and in Sadi's composing his *Bustan* ('The Orchard'). Included in the Introduction are the Life and Times and Poetry of Sana'i and a history of the various poetic forms that he wrote in. Selected Bibliography. The correct rhyme-structure has been kept as well as the beauty and meaning of these immortal poems. 136 Pages.

THE ROSE GARDEN OF MYSTERY: SHABISTARI
Translation by Paul Smith. Introduction by E.H. Whinfield & Paul Smith
The Rose Garden of Mystery was composed as a 1000 couplet long *masnavi* poem in the form of questions and answers on spiritual matters by Mahmud Shabistari of Tabriz in 1317 at the request of his Spiritual Master. Since then it has been regarded as one of the finest books on Sufism. E.G. Browne in his classic work, 'History of Persian Literature' calls this book "On the whole, one of the best manuals of Sufi theosophy that exists." Rev. John A. Subhan in his 'Sufism, Its Saints and Shrines' states, "We know little about the life of the author... But his work is important out of all comparison with the importance of the author because it is a compendium of Sufi terminology in the form of question and answer."
The correct rhyme-structure has been kept in this complete, modern translation, as well as the beauty and meaning of this beautiful, mystical, poem. Selected Bibliography. Pages 182

RUDAKI: SELECTED POEMS
Translation, Introduction & Notes by Paul Smith
Abu 'Abd Allah Ja'far ibn Muhammad Rudaki (858-941) the 'father of Persian Poetry' and possibly the *ruba'i*, was born in the village of Rudak

near Samarkand. First a wandering 'dervish' poet/minstrel he later served at the court of the Samanids of Bokhara. Nasr ibn Ahmad summoned him to his court and he prospered there amassing great wealth. He had 200 slaves in his retinue... and 400 camels carried his belongings when he travelled. In 937 he fell out of favour at court (and was blinded at this time as some commentators suggest) after the death of the prime-minister who had supported him. His life ended in abject poverty, forgotten by the world at that time, perhaps the reason why so much of his vast output of 1,300,000 couplets, only 75 *rubai's, ghazals, qasidas* and *qit'as survive* (most are here translated, the most published). Rudaki's poetry is about the passage of time, old age, death, fortune's fickleness, importance of the matters of the heart, the need to be happy. Although he praised kings, nobles and heroes... his greatest love was knowledge and experience. The Introduction contains: Persian Poetry, A New Beginning; The Life, Times and Poetry of Rudaki; The Various Forms in the Poetry of Rudaki and a Selected Bibliography. The correct rhyme-structure has been kept in this modern translation, as well as the beauty and meaning of these beautiful poems. 140 pages.

SADI: SELECTED POEMS
Translation, Introduction & Notes by Paul Smith
Sadi of Shiraz, along with Hafiz, Nizami & Rumi is considered one of the great mystical and romantic poets of Iran. His masterpieces, *The Rose Garden* and *The Bustan* (Orchard) have been a major influence in the East and West for the past 700 years. His *Divan* of *ghazals* are still much loved by Iranians. His *ruba'is* have also been an influence on the poets that followed him. Here is a large selection of his *ghazals, ruba'is* and *masnavis*. Included is a long Introduction on his Life and Times and Poetry. There is also a Selected Bibliography and Glossary of Sufi Symbols. The correct rhyme-structure has been kept in this modern translation, as well as the beauty and meaning of these beautiful poems. 207 pages.

JAMI: SELECTED POEMS
Translation, Introduction by Paul Smith
Jami (1414-1493), is still considered the last great poet of the Classical Period (10th-15th C.) of Persian Poetry is mostly known for his masterpiece seven *masnavi* epics... including his masterpieces Joseph and Zulaikh... also Layla and Majnun, Chain of Gold and Book of the Wisdom of Alexander.
He also composed three *Divans* consisting of *ghazals rubai's* and other profound, mystical poems. Here is the largest number of his *ghazals* and *ruba'is* translated into English and a good selection from most of his

masnavis. Included in the Introduction… the life of Jami and a chapter of Sufism in Persian Poetry and a chapter on the various forms of poetry he used and a Selected Bibliography. The correct rhyme-structure is kept as well as the beauty and meaning of these beautiful, mystical poems. 164 Pages.

NIZAMI: SELECTED POEMS
Translation & Introduction by Paul Smith
Nizami (d. 1208) is a true Sufi Master Poet who is most famous for his six books in *masnavi* form: *The Treasury of the Mysteries, Layla and Majnun, Khosrau and Shirin, The Seven Portraits* and his two books on Alexander. He also composed a *Divan* of approximately 20,000 couplets mostly in *ghazals* and *ruba'is*… tragically only 200 couplets survive. His influence on Attar, Rumi, Sadi, Hafiz and Jami and all others that followed was profound. Here is the largest number of his *ghazals* and *ruba'is* and *qasidas* translated into English and a good selection from his *masnavis*. Included in the Introduction… the life and Times and Poetry of Nizami and on the various forms of poetry he used and a Selected Bibliography. The correct rhyme-structure has been kept as well as the beauty and meaning of these beautiful, mystical poems. 235 pages.

RUBA'IYAT OF BEDIL
Translation & Introduction by Paul Smith
Mirza Abdul-Qader Bedil (1644-1721) is one of the most respected poets originally from Afghanistan. In the early 17th century, his family moved from Balkh to India, to live under the Mughul dynasty. He was born and educated near Patna. In his later life he spent time travelling and visiting ancestral lands. His writings in Persian are extensive, being one of the creators of the 'Indian style'. He had complicated views on the nature of God, heavily influenced by the Sufis. Bedil's 16 books of poetry contain nearly 147,000 couplets with over 3600 poems that are *ruba'is*. He is now considered a great later master of this form. The correct rhyme-structure is kept as well as the beauty and meaning of these beautiful, often mystical poems. 134 pages.

BEDIL: SELECTED POEMS
Translation & Introduction by Paul Smith
Mirza Abdul-Qader Bedil (1644-1721) is one of the most respected poets from Afghanistan. In the early 17th century, his family moved from Balkh to India, to live under the Mughul dynasty. He was born and educated near Patna. In his later life he spent time travelling and visiting ancestral lands.

His writings in Persian are extensive, being one of the creators of the 'Indian style'. Bedil's 16 books of poetry contain nearly 147,000 couplets. With Ghalib he is considered a master of the complicated 'Indian Style' of the *ghazal*. He had complicated views on the nature of God, heavily influenced by the Sufis. The correct rhyme-structure has been kept as well as the beauty and meaning of these beautiful and often mystical poems. Pages... 144

ANVARI: SELECTED POEMS
Translation & Introduction by Paul Smith
Ahad-ud-din Anvari Abeverdi (1126-1189) was a court poet of the Seljuk sultans. Jami composed a *ruba'i* where he names him, along with Firdausi and Sadi as one of the 'three apostles' of Persian poetry. He was also a celebrated astronomer, mathematician and scientist who admitted he gave them up for the more lucrative occupation of ... a court poet, that he later rejected twenty years before his death for a life of seclusion and contemplation. He is renowned for his delightful wittiness that can be found in many of his *ruba'is* and *qit'as and ghazals*. He is one of the greatest Persian masters of the *qasida* and his one called 'The Tears of Khurasan' is considered his masterpieces. He is known for his sense of humour and sometimes obscenity. He created a new kind of poetry by using the conversational language of his time in simple words and expressions. The correct rhyme-structure has been kept as well as the beauty and meaning of these beautiful, poems. 156 pages.

RUBA'IYAT OF 'IRAQI
Translation & Introduction by Paul Smith
'Iraqi (1213-1289) was the author of a *Divan* of spiritual *ghazals* and *ruba'is* and the famous work in prose and poetry... *Lama'at*, 'Divine Flashes'... a classic of Sufi Mysticism. He was born in Hamadan in western Persia and as a child learnt the *Koran* by heart. He travelled from Persia to India with dervishes where he stayed for 25 years. It is said that on his travels he met Rumi. His grave is in Damascus beside that of another great Perfect Master and poet Ibn al-'Arabi. When seeing these graves a pilgrim stated, "That ('Iraqi) is the Persian Gulf and this (Ibn al-'Arabi) is the Arabian Sea." The correct rhyme-structure has been kept as well as the beauty and meaning of these beautiful, mystical poems. 116 pages.

THE WISDOM OF IBN YAMIN: SELECTED POEMS
Translation & Introduction Paul Smith
Amir Fakhr al-Din Mahmud, or Ibn Yamin (1286-1367), was born in Turkistan. His father was a poet who taught him the craft and left his son wealthy and the role of the court-poet in Khurasan. Ibn Yamin was taken captive when war broke out in 1342 and his complete *Divan* of poems was destroyed. He was a master of the form of the *qi'ta*. He is now as he was then, famous for his down-to-earth wisdom. Hafiz was probably influenced by his poems. During the last 25 years of his life he composed a further 5000 couplets on top of those he remembered. Here is the largest translation of his poems published in correct-rhyming, meaningful English. Introduction: Life & Times & Poetry, Forms in which he wrote, Bibliography. 155 pages.

NESIMI: SELECTED POEMS
Translation & Introduction by Paul Smith
Nesimi (1369-1417) is considered one of the greatest mystical poets of the late 14th and early 15th centuries and one of the most prominent early masters in Turkish/Azerbaijani literary history. For Nesimi at the centre of Creation there was God, who bestowed His Light on man. Through sacrifice and self-perfection, man can become one with Him. As a direct result of his beliefs he was skinned alive. His tomb in Aleppo remains an important place of pilgrimage to this day. His work consists of two collections of poems, one in Persian and the most important in Turkish that consists of 250-300 *ghazels* and about 175 *roba'is*. After his death his work continued to exercise an influence on Turkish language poets and authors. The 600th anniversary of Nesimi's birth was celebrated worldwide by UNESCO. The Introduction is on his Life & Times & Poetry and the Forms in which he wrote. The correct rhyme-structure has been kept as well as the beauty and meaning of these beautiful, mystical poems. 210 pages

ROBA'IYAT OF NESIMI
Translation & Introduction by Paul Smith
Nesimi (1369-1417) is one of the great spiritual poets of the late 14th and early 15th centuries and one of the masters in Turkish/Azerbaijani literary history. For Nesimi at the centre of Creation there was God, who bestowed His Light on man. Through sacrifice and self-perfection, man can become one with Him. His poems were considered heresy and he skinned alive as punishment. His tomb in Aleppo remains an important place of pilgrimage to this day. His Turkish *roba'iyat* consists of about 175 *roba'is*, 13 in Persian (most are here translated). The 600th anniversary of Nesimi's

birth was celebrated by UNESCO. The correct rhyme-structure has been kept as well as the beauty and meaning of these beautiful, mystical poems. 145 pages

SHAH NI'MATULLAH: SELECTED POEMS
Translation & Introduction by Paul Smith
Shah Ni'matullah Vali (1330-1431) was the founder of an order of Sufis that is today the largest in Iran. As well as a Sufi Master he was a poet who at times used 'Sayyid' as his *takhallus* or pen-name. He was influenced by Ibn 'Arabi and Hafiz. He came from Aleppo and after studies travelled in Egypt, Morocco, Mecca (where he met his Spiritual Master Abdullah Yafi'i). He built a monastery in Mahan near Kirman and lived there until his death. He composed many prose works on Sufism and his *Divan* contains over 13,000 couplets, mostly *ghazals* and *ruba'is*. This is the largest selection of his poems published in English. Introduction is on his Life & Times & Poetry and the Forms in which he wrote and on Sufism & Poetry. The correct rhyme-structure has been kept as well as the meaning of these beautiful, enlightened poems. Glossary, bibliography. 168 pages

AMIR KHUSRAU: SELECTED POEMS
Translation & Introduction by Paul Smith
Amir Khusrau (1253-1324), the 'Parrot of India' was born at Patigali near the Ganges in India. At the age of thirty-six he was poet-laureate, serving many sultans. He was not only fluent in Persian, in which he composed the majority of his 92 books, but also in Arabic, Hindi and Sanskrit. He composed ten long *masnavis*, five *Divans* of *ghazals* and other poems and many prose works. He was a Master musician and invented the *sitar*. The Perfect Master Nizam ud-din took him as his disciple and eventually he became God-realized. He rebelled against narrow spirituality and helped redefine the true Sufi way. He was a profound influence on Hafiz and is seen as the link between Sadi and Hafiz in updating the form and content of the *ghazal* and eroticising it. This is the largest selection of his poems in English. Introduction is on his Life & Times & Poetry and the Forms in which he wrote and on Sufism & Poetry. The correct rhyme-structure has been kept and the meaning of these beautiful, enlightened poems. 201 pages

A WEALTH OF POETS: Persian Poetry at the Courts of Sultan Mahmud in Ghazneh & Sultan Sanjar in Ganjeh (998-1158)
Translations, Introduction and Notes by Paul Smith
CONTENTS: Persian Poetry: A New Beginning... 7, Sultan Mahmud: His Life, Times and Poets 9. Sultan Sanjar: His Life, Times & Poets... 17.

The Various Forms in Persian Poetry… 22, Sufism in Persian Poetry… 31.
THE POETS: Poets at the Court of Sultan Mahmud… page 35,
Sultan Mahmud 37, Umarah 39, Kisa'i 41, Firdausi 44, Farrukhi 55, Asjadi 67, Manuchirhri 69, Poet-laureate Unsuri 75, Asadi 82.
Poets at the Court of Sultan Sanjar… page 89, Poet-laureate Mu'izzi 91, Sabir 101, Mahsati 105, Jabali 116, Vatvat 120, Anvari 124.
The correct rhyme-structures have been kept and the meaning of these often beautiful, challenging, powerful and sometimes mystical poems. 158 pages

SHIMMERING JEWELS: Anthology of Poetry Under the Reigns of the Mughal Emperors of India (1526-1857)
Translations, Introductions, Etc. by Paul Smith
CONTENTS: The Mughal Empire… Page 7, Emperor Babur… 14, Emperor Humayun… 19, Emperor Akbar… 31, Emperor Jahangir… 44, Emperor Shah Jahan… 50, Emperor Aurangzeb… 57, Emperor Bahadur Shah Zafar… 71. Sufis & Dervishes: Their Art and Use of Poetry… 78, The Main Forms in Persian, Urdu & Pushtu Poetry of the Indian Sub-Continent… 81 Poets in the Reign of Babur… 91, Babur 93, Wafa'i 96, Farighi 97, Haqiri 98. Poets in the Reign of Humayun… 99, Humayun 102, Kamran 104, Nadiri 106, Bayram 107. Poets in the Reign of Akbar… 109, Akbar 111, Ghazali 113, Maili 116, Kahi 117, Faizi 119, Urfi 122, Nami 127, Hayati 130, Qutub Shah 132, Naziri 135. Poets in the Reign of Jahangir… 137, Jahangir 139, Rahim 140, Talib 142, Shikebi 160, Tausani 161, Qasim 162. Poets in the Reign of Shah Jahan… 163, Qudsi 165, Sa'ib 168, Kalim 172. Poets in Reign of Aurangzeb… 177, Dara Shikoh 179, Mullah Shah 186, Sarmad 189, Khushal 199, Nasir Ali 213, Makhfi 215, Wali 239, Bedil 243. Poets in the Reign of Bahadur Shah Zafar… 251, Zafar 253, Zauq 260, Ghalib 266, Momin 275, Shefta 280, Dagh 283. The correct rhyme-structures have been kept and the meaning of these often beautiful, powerful and sometimes mystical poems. Pages 292.

RAHMAN BABA: SELECTED POEMS
Translation & Introduction by Paul Smith
Rahman Baba (1652 to 1711) is considered the greatest Sufi Pashtun poet to compose poems, mainly *ghazals,* in the Pushtu language. Born in Mohmand region of Afghanistan near Peshawar he was called 'The Nightingale of Peshawar'. This was a time of struggle and hardship and in the midst of the turmoil he was an excellent student with a natural gift for poetry.
He eventually questioned the value of such pursuits and withdrew from the world, dedicating himself to prayer and devotion. In solitary worship he began to write again and his poetry spread. Religious figures used it to

inspire the devout, political leaders to inspire the independence movement. His *Divan* is 343 poems… *ghazals* and a few *qasidas* and *mukhammas*. Introduction is on his Life & Times & Poetry and the Forms in which he wrote and on Sufism & Poetry. The correct rhyme-structure is kept as well as the meaning of these beautiful, enlightened poems. 139 pages

RUBA'IYAT OF DARA SHIKOH
Translation & Introduction by Paul Smith
Dara Shikoh (1615-1659) was the oldest son of Emperor Shah Jahan and was known to be a loving husband, a good son and loving father. He was a fine poet, his poems having the influence of Sufism to which he was dedicated. He used 'Qadiri' as his *takhallus* or pen-name. His *Divan* of *ghazals*, *ruba'is* and *qasidas* in Persian was not the only work he left behind, his five prose works on Sufism and mysticism are popular in India even today. His *Majma al-Bahrain* or *The Mingling of the Two Oceans* is an explanation of the mystical sameness of Sufism and Vedanta. He also translated the *Upanishads, Bhagavad Gita and Yoga-Vasishta* into Persian. After he was defeated after leading an uprising against his cruel, fundamentalist brother Emperor Aurangzeb and was brutally killed in 1659. The correct rhyme-structure has been kept and the meaning of these beautiful, powerful mystical poems. This is the largest translation of his poems into English. 120 pages

ANTHOLOGY OF POETRY OF THE CHISHTI SUFI ORDER
Translations & Introduction by Paul Smith
The Chishti Order is a Sufi order within the mystic branches of Islam which was founded in Chisht, a small town near Herat, Afghanistan about 930 A.D. The Chishti Order is known for its emphasis on love, tolerance, and openness. The Master & Perfect Master Poets: Mu'in ud-din Chishti, Baba Farid, Nizam –ud-din Auliya, Amir Khusrau, Dara Shikoh, Inayat Khan, Khadim & others. Introduction on the Chishti Order of Sufism and the Spiritual forms of the Master Poets of this famous Order of the Indian Sub-Continent. The correct rhyme-structures have been kept and the meaning of these often beautiful, powerful and always spiritual poems. Pages 300.

POEMS OF MAJNUN (Qays Ibn al-Mulawwah 664-668)
Translation & Introduction by Paul Smith
Qays was a youth, a Bedouin poet in the seventh century of the Bani Amir tribe in the Najd desert. He fell in love with Layla from the same tribe whom he was denied. (It is said that Shakespeare got his Romeo & Juliet from their tragic love story). Most of his recorded poetry was composed

before his descent into madness *(mast)* then through a Perfect Master... his spiritual unification with his beloved. Nizami's famous telling of their tale came from this collected poems *(Divan)* and other sources. Hundreds of other Persian, Turkish and Urdu poets imitated him or wrote their own versions of the story of the height of human love that became Divine. Here in the form of the *qit'a* in which they were composed, is the largest collection of poems put into English. Four Appendixes. 220 pages.

RUBA'IYAT OF ANSARI
Translation & Introduction by Paul Smith
One of the greatest mystical poets and Perfect Masters of all time, Abdullah Ansari... who passed from this world 1089 in Herat was most famous for his biographical dictionary on saints and Sufi masters and his much loved collection of inspiring prayers, the *Munajat* among many works in Persian and Arabic. His *ruba'is* appear throughout his works. The correct rhyme-structure has been kept and the meaning of these beautiful, powerful, mystical poems. This is the largest translation of his *ruba'is* into English. 183 pages

RUBA'IYAT OF SHAH NI'MATULLAH
Translation & Introduction by Paul Smith
Shah Ni'matullah Vali (1330-1431) was the founder of an order of Sufis that is today the largest in Iran. As well as a Sufi Master he was a poet who at times used 'Sayyid' as his *takhallus* or pen-name. He was influenced by Ibn 'Arabi and Hafiz. He came from Aleppo and after studies travelled in Egypt, Morocco, Mecca (where he met his Spiritual Master Abdullah Yafi'i). He built a monastery in Mahan near Kirman and lived there until his death. He composed many prose works on Sufism and his *Divan* contains over 13,000 couplets, mostly *ghazals* and *ruba'is*. This is the largest selection of his *ruba'is* published in English. Introduction is on his Life & Times & Poetry and the meaning of Sufi poetry and a History of the Form and Function of the *Ruba'i*. The correct rhyme-structure has been kept as well as the meaning of these beautiful, enlightened poems. Glossary, bibliography. 125 pages

ANSARI: SELECTED POEMS
Translation & Introduction by Paul Smith
One of the greatest mystical poets and Perfect Masters of all time, Abdullah Ansari... who passed from this world 1089 in Herat was most famous for his biographical dictionary on saints and Sufi masters and his much loved collection of inspiring prayers, the *Munajat* among many works

in Persian and Arabic. His *ruba'is* appear throughout his works and he composed three *Divans* in which his *ghazals* are in the majority. Here is a fine selection of them and a *qasida*. The correct rhyme-structure has been kept and the meaning of these beautiful, powerful, mystical poems. This is the largest translation of his poems into English. 156 pages

BABA FARID: SELECTED POEMS
Translation & Introduction by Paul Smith
The father of Punjabi poetry Baba Farid (1173-1266) was born in the Punjab. Khwaja Bakhtiar Kaki was Baba Farid's Spiritual Master. Kaki met Mu'in ud-din Chishti at Baghdad and became his disciple. The king at Delhi, Balban, welcomed Farid in Delhi. His daughter married Farid. Baba Farid, the Sufi Master poet laureate from Punjab is famous for his wise and spiritual couplets *(slokas)*... 112 of them are in the bible of the Sikhs (whom he influenced) the *Guru Granth,* and 128 are translated here with the correct rhyme-structure and meaning. Hospitals and factories and even a town named after him. 164 pages.

POETS OF THE NI'MATULLAH SUFI ORDER
Translations & Introduction by Paul Smith
Shah Ni'matullah (1330-1431) was the founder of an order of Sufis that is today one of the largest in Iran and around the world. As well as a Sufi Master he was a poet who inspired many Spiritual Masters and Sufi Poets over the following 500 years to follow his example.
CONTENTS: The Ni'matullah Sufi Order... page 7, Sufis & Dervishes: Their Art & Use of Poetry... 10, Forms of Poetry used by the Ni'matullah Poets... 26, Selected Bibliography... 35, Glossary... 36
The Poets...Shah Ni'matullah... 39, Bushaq... 85, Kasim Anwar... 117, Shah Da'i... 145, Nur 'Ali Shah... 167, Bibi Hayati... 178, Rida 'Ali Shah... 209, Muzaffar 'Ali Shah... 221, Khusrawi... 230, Munis 'Ali Shah... 236.
The correct rhyme-structures have been kept and the meaning of these beautiful, powerful and mystical poems. This is the largest translation of their poems into English. 244 pages.

MU'IN UD-DIN CHISHTI: SELECTED POEMS
Translation & Introduction by Paul Smith
Mu'in ud-din Chishti (1141-1230) was also known as *Gharib Nawaz* or 'Benefactor of the Poor', he is the most famous Sufi saint of the Chishti Order of the Indian Subcontinent. He also composed many *ghazals*. In his book *Pre Mughal Persian in Hindustan,* Muhammad 'Abdu'l Ghani states... "He was the greatest lyric poet of his age. His style is exuberant

and precise at once. His poems are a storehouse of transcendental thoughts beautifully ordered and forcefully expressed. There is always a sense of pious serenity and joy in his verses which are teeming with Divine Love... his poetry resembles closely that of Hafiz... He takes his readers along with him solely to spiritual ecstasy and gives them a peep into the ethereal world..." Today, hundreds of thousands of people... Muslims, Hindus, Christians and others take grace from his tomb and poems. This is the largest selection of his *ghazals* translated into English in the correct form and meaning. 171 pages.

QASIDAH BURDAH: THE THREE POEMS OF THE PROPHET'S MANTLE
Translations & Introduction by Paul Smith

Ka'b ibn Zuhair (died 7th century A.D.) was a famous poet who at first opposed Prophet Muhammad. Finally, he secretly went to Medina and approached the Prophet to ask if one who repented and embraced the faith would be forgiven. Mohammed answered yes and the poet asked, "Even Ka'b ibn Zuhair?" When he affirmed this, Ka'b revealed his identity and read a poem, his *Banat Suad* (of 55 couplets), which would become his most famous poem. As a reward Prophet Mohammed took off his mantle (cloak) and put it on Ka'b's shoulders. The second 'Mantle' *qasida* (ode) of praise for Mohammed was composed by the eminent Sufi, Imam al-Busiri (1210-1297). The poem (161 couplets) is famous mainly in the Sunni Muslim world. It is entirely in praise of Prophet Mohammed, who is said to have cured the poet of paralysis by appearing to him in a dream and wrapping him in a mantle. The third poet of the 'Mantle' was Ahmed Shawqi (1869 - 1932) the great Arabic Poet-Laureate, an Egyptian poet and dramatist who pioneered the modern Egyptian literary movement, most notably introducing the genre of poetic epics to the Arabic literary tradition. His 'Mantle' *qasida* is 190 couplets. The correct rhyme-structure has been kept and the meaning of these beautiful, powerful, spiritual poems. Pages 116

RUBA'IYAT OF ANVARI
Translation & Introduction by Paul Smith

Ahad-ud-din Anvari Abeverdi (1126-1189) was a court poet of the Seljuk sultans. Jami composed a *ruba'i* where he names him, along with Firdausi and Sadi as one of the 'three apostles' of Persian poetry. He was also a celebrated astronomer, mathematician and scientist who gave them up for the more lucrative occupation of... a court poet, that he rejected twenty years before his death for a life of contemplation. He is renowned for his delightful wittiness that can be found in many of his *ruba'is* and *qit'as* and *ghazals*. He is known for his sense of humour and sometimes obscenity. He created a new kind of poetry by using the conversational language of his time. Introduction includes: The Life, Times and Poetry of Anvari, Sufis & Dervishes: Their Art & Use of Poetry, The Ruba'i: Its Form, Use & History. The correct rhyme-structure has been kept as well as the beauty and meaning of these poems. 74 pages.

'IRAQI: SELECTED POEMS
Translation & Introduction by Paul Smith
'Iraqi (1213-1289) was the author of a *Divan* of spiritual *ghazals* and *ruba'is* and the famous work in prose and poetry... *Lama'at,* 'Divine Flashes'... a classic of Sufi Mysticism. He was born in Hamadan in western Persia and as a child learnt the *Koran* by heart. He travelled from Persia to India with dervishes where he stayed for 25 years. It is said that on his travels he met Rumi. His grave is in Damascus beside that of another great Perfect Master and poet Ibn al-'Arabi. When seeing these graves a pilgrim stated, "That ('Iraqi) is the Persian Gulf and this (Ibn al- 'Arabi) is the Arabian Sea." Introduction: The Life & Times & Poems of 'Iraqi, Selected Bibliography, Forms in Classical Persian Poetry Used by 'Iraqi. *Rubai's, Ghazals, Qasida, Masnavis, Tarji-band.* The correct rhyme-structure has been kept as well as the beauty and meaning of these beautiful, mystical poems. 158 pages.

MANSUR HALLAJ: SELECTED POEMS
Translation & Introduction by Paul Smith
The Perfect Master, poet & martyr, Husayn Mansur al-Hallaj (died 919), was born in Shiraz and tortured and executed in Baghdad for declaring: "I am the Truth *(Anal Haq)."* Much has been written about his famous (and infamous) statement, but few of his powerful, often mysteries and always deeply conscious and spiritual poems in Arabic have been translated before from his *Divan* into English, and in the poetic form in which they were composed. The Introduction contains: The Life, Times and Works of Mansur Hallaj, The Perfect Master *(Qutub),* 'Anal-Haq' or 'I am the Truth' of Mansur Hallaj, Four Master Poets of Baghdad who influenced Hallaj, Sufis & Dervishes: Their Art & Use of Poetry. There is a wide selection of his *qit'as, ghazals, ruba'is, qasidas.* Included are two appendixes: A Selection of Poetry from the Persian, Turkish & Pashtu poetry about or influenced by him, and the *Tawasin* of Mansur al-Hallaj. Translated by Aish Abd Ar-Rahman At-Tarjumana. Pages 209.

RUBA'IYAT OF BABA AFZAL
Translation & Introduction by Paul Smith
Baba Afzal (1186-1256) came from Maraq near Kashan. He is the author of many Persian works on philosophical and metaphysical subjects and translated the Arabic version of Aristotle's 'The Book of the Soul' into Persian. He was a Sufi and the author of about 500 mystical and at times controversial *ruba'is* some that have been mistakenly identified as Khayyam's. Some of the themes in these include warnings about the futility of involvement with the things of the world, correspondence between microcosm and macrocosm and self-knowledge as the goal of human existence. He is one of the greatest poets among the philosophers of Islam. Introduction includes: The Life, Times & Work of Baba Afzal, Sufis: Their Art & Use of Poetry, The *Ruba'i*: Its Form, Use & History. The correct rhyme-structure has been kept as well as the beauty and meaning of these poems. 178 pages.

RIBALD POEMS OF THE SUFI POETS
Sana'i, Anvari, Mahsati, Rumi, Sadi, Obeyd Zakani
Translations, Introductions Paul Smith
Some of the greatest of the Persian Sufi poets composed ribald and at times 'obscene' poems for satirical and often (as in the case of Rumi) for teaching some spiritual truth or moral. Here is a wide-ranging selection of the greatest of them from the eleventh to the fourteenth century. Here are at times hilarious, witty, weird, and erotic and obscene poems in most of the various forms of classical Persian poetry… the *ghazal,* the *ruba'i,* the *masnavi,* the *qit'a,* the *qasida* and the *tarji-band.* 190 pages.

RUMI: SELECTIONS FROM HIS *MASNAVI*
Translation & Introduction by Paul Smith
The *masnavi* is the form used in Persian and other languages to write epic ballads or romances and it is essentially a Persian invention. The most famous poems written in this form are the 'Shahnama' (Book of the Kings) of Firdausi, the 'Enclosed Garden of the Truth' of Sana'i, the 'Five Treasures' of Nizami, the 'Conference of the Birds' and 'The Book of God' and many others by 'Attar, the 'Seven Thrones' of Jami, the ten *masnavis* of Amir Khusrau and of course the greatest of them all… the *'Masnavi'* of Rumi. Many *masnavis* by the great Perfect Master Poets were of a Sufi/Dervish mystical nature. Included in this volume is a chapter on The Life, Times & Poetry of Rumi and one on the history of the *masnavi* in Persian poetry by the various masters in this form with translations of their works up until Rumi. From Rumi's *Masnavi* are his Introduction to the 6 volumes and the first three Tales in full and excerpts from the whole work,

including some of his ribald tales. Selected Bibliography. The correct rhyme-form of the *masnavi* has been kept in all the translations. 260 pages.

WINE OF LOVE: AN ANTHOLOGY,
Wine in the Poetry of Arabia, Persia, Turkey & the Indian Sub-Continent from Pre-Islamic Times to the Present
Translations & Introduction by Paul Smith
CONTENTS Arabic Poetry 7, Persian Poetry 11, Turkish Poetry 13, Pushtu Poetry 15, Urdu Poetry 17, The Main Forms in Arabic, Persian, Turkish, Pushtu & Urdu Poetry 19, Wine in Sufi Poetry 29, Arabic Poetry... 37, Ima'-ul-Qays 39, Antara 47, Tarafa 59, Amru 72, Labid 80, Ka'b 92, Omar Ibn abi Rabi'a 96, Majnun 98, Rabi'a of Basra 101, Abu Nuwas 106, Bayazid Bastami 114, Al-Mutanabbi 116, Al-Ma'arri 131, Gilani 134, Suhrawadi 137, Ibn al-Farid 140, Ibn 'Arabi 145, Al-Shushtari 148. Persian Poetry... 151, Abu Shakur 153, Junaidi 155, Rudaki 157, Agachi 172, Rabi'a Balkhi 174, Daqiqi 177, Umarah 181, Kisa'i 183, Farrukhi 185, Asjadi 193, Minuchihri 195, Unsuri 198, Abu Sa'id 201, Baba Kuhi 203, Qatran 205, Ansari 207, Al-Ghazali 212, Mas'ud Sa'd 214, Mu'izzi 216, Omar Khayyam 219, Sana'I 227, Sabir 232, Mahsati 235, Jabali 238, Vatvat 240, Anvari 242, Falaki 246, Hasan Ghaznavi 249, Athir 252, Mujir 255, Khaqani 257, Mu'in 266, Zahir 274, Nizami 278, Ruzbihan 284, 'Attar 286, Auhad ud-din Kermani 292, Kamal ad-din 294, Baba Afzal 297, Rumi 299, Sadi 310, 'Iraqi 323, Humam 335, Amir Khusray 337, Hasan Dihlavi 347, Khaju 351, Obeyd Zakani 353, Emad 361, Salman 366, Shahin 371, Hafiz 374, Ruh Attar 396, Haydar 401, Junaid Shirazi 404, Jahan Khatun 406, Maghribi 413, Bushaq 415, Kasim Anwar 419, Shah Ni'matu'llah 422, Jami 425, Ahli 428, Helali 430, Fighani 432, Babur 435, Ghazali 437, Urfi 439, Lotfali Suratgar 493, Rahi 495. Turkish Poetry... 497, Ahmed Yesevi 499, Yunus Emre 502, Kadi Burhan-ud-din 507, Nesimi 509, Mihri 515, Necati 518, Pir Sultan 523, Khayali 535, Fuzuli 528, Baqi 535, Huda'I 539, Nef'I 541, Yahya 544, Na'ila 546, Nabi 548, Nedim 550, Fitnet 553, Galib 555, Leyla Khanim 562. Pushtu Poetry... 565, Mirza 567, Khushal 570, Ashraf Khan 578, Abdul-Khadir 580, Rahman Baba 585, Khwaja Mohammad 588, Shaida 592. Urdu Poetry... 595, Wali 587, Sauda 599, Dard 601, Nazir 603, Mir 606, Zauq 610, Ghalib 612, Momin 619, Dagh 621, Shad 623, Iqbal 625, Ashgar 629, Josh 631, Jigar 633, Huma 637, Firaq 641, Faiz 643. 645 pages.

GHALIB: SELECTED POEMS
Translation & Introduction by Paul Smith
Mirza Asadullah Beg (1797-1869), known as Ghalib (conqueror), was born in the city of Agra of parents with Turkish aristocratic ancestry. When he was

only five his father Abdullah Beg Khan died in a battle while working under Rao Raja Bakhtwar. Ghalib's fame came to him posthumously. He had himself remarked during his lifetime that although his age had ignored his greatness, it would be recognised by later generations. History has vindicated his claim. Ghalib wrote beautiful *ghazals* and other poems in Persian... over 250 (many are translated here) but is more famous for his *ghazals* written in Urdu. Before Ghalib, the Urdu *ghazal* was primarily an expression of anguished love, but Ghalib expressed his philosophy and cynicism on God and other subjects. His Urdu *Divan* contains 263 *ghazals* and a small number of *ruba'is, masnavis, qasidas* and *qit'as*. There have been many movies based on his life made in India and Pakistan where his popularity has never flagged. Introduction on his Life, Poetry and Times and the Forms of Poetry he wrote in. The correct rhyme-structure has been kept as well as the beauty and meaning of these poems. Pages 200.

THE ENLIGHTENED SAYINGS OF HAZRAT 'ALI
The Right Hand of the Poet
Translation & Introduction by Paul Smith
Hazrat 'Ali (598-661) was Prophet Mohammed's nephew, son-in-law and favourite and was the first Imam of the Shi'ites and the fourth of the true caliphs of the Sunnis. Sufi Masters believe in Ali as one of the 'Seven Great Ones' in the first generation of teachers and many in orders of Dervishes trace their spiritual ancestry back to him. Hazrat Ali's sayings are published as *Nahj al-Balagh* or 'The Peak of Experience'... a treasury of wisdom and divine grace. It is said that he wrote the original *Koran* in his own blood as Prophet Mohammed gave it. He also composed a *Divan* of enlightened poetry and one of his important, profound *ghazals* is translated in the Introduction to this book. Pages 260.

HAFIZ: TONGUE OF THE HIDDEN
A Selection of *Ghazals* from his *Divan*
Translation & Introduction Paul Smith
This is the completely revised third edition of a selection of Hafiz's *ghazals* from his Divan his masterpiece of 791 *ghazals, masnavis, rubais* and other poems/songs. The spiritual and historical and human content is here in understandable, beautiful poetry: the correct rhyme-structure has been achieved, without intruding, in readable English. In the Introduction his life story is told in great detail; his spirituality is explored, the form and function of his poetry, Glossary, Selected Bibliography. 133 pages. Third Edition.

HAFIZ: THE SUN OF SHIRAZ
Essays, Talks, Projects on the Immortal Poet
Paul Smith
CONTENTS: Introduction by Richard Lee; The Life of Hafiz; Hafiz's Influence on the East & the West, The English Translations of Hafiz; Hafiz and His Translator, Sufism and God; Poetry, Life and Times of Hafiz of Shiraz; UNESCO and Hafiz; Hafiz for Our Time; Preface to Original Divan. 249 pages

~ HAFIZ: A DAYBOOK ~
Translation & Introduction by Paul Smith
Hafiz is considered by many of the world's foremost poets, mystics, artists and writers to be the greatest poet of all time. Hafiz was not only a great poet, he became a Perfect Master or enlightened being, whose wisdom and insights into the everyday and mystical path are such that it is said that one can gain spiritual advancement by reading his book. During the past six centuries he has inspired and influenced the world of literature, philosophy, mysticism and all aspects of art: poetry, painting and music in the east and the west. His life was for mankind and his work to be shared with the world. Through his example we can learn how to prepare for unprecedented change. Without doubt, he is one of the greatest human beings since time began. His *Divan* has been loved by many millions of people. To this day it is used as an oracle and spiritual guide and in this Daybook one can use his couplets on a daily basis or open them at random for inspiration and advice. 375 pages.

~* RUMI* ~ A Daybook
Translation & Introduction by Paul Smith
The great Sufi Master and poet Jalal-ud-din Rumi was born in 1207 in Balkh. Rumi's love and his great longing for the Perfect Master Shams –e Tabriz found expression in music, dance, songs and poems in his collection of poems/songs or *Divan*. This vast work included thousands of *ghazals* and other poetic forms and nearly two thousand *ruba'is* which he would compose for many years, before he became a God-realised Perfect Master himself and also afterwards. Most of the poems in this Daybook are taken from his collection of *ruba'is*, but there are also selected couplets from his *ghazals* and his profound *Masnavi*. Introduction on his Life and Times, Selected Bibliography. The correct rhyme-structure has been kept in all 366 poems. Pages 383.

SUFI POETRY OF INDIA ~ A Daybook~
Translation & Introduction by Paul Smith
This is a Daybook of Sufi and Dervish Poetry of India in various poetic forms. Over 400 inspirational and spiritually helpful and beautiful poems to inspire and make your day. CONTENTS: The Poets, Sufis & Dervishes: Their Art and Use of Poetry, Glossary, The Main Forms in Persian, Punjabi, Hindi, Kashmiri, Sindhi and Urdu Sufi and Dervish Poetry of India, Selected Bibliography... THE POETS: Mu'in ud-din Chishti, Baba Farid, Amir Khusrau, Hasan Dihlavi, Lalla Ded, Kabir, Qutub Shah, Dara Shikoh, Sarmad, Sultan Bahu, Nasir Ali, Makhfi, Wali, Bedil, Bulleh Shah, Shah Latif, Ali Haider, Sauda, Dard, Nazir, Mir, Sachal Sarmast, Aatish, Zafar, Zauq, Ghalib, Dabir, Anees, Hali, Farid, Shad, Iqbal, Inayat Khan, Asghar, Jigar, Huma, Firaq, Josh. Pages 404.

~ SUFI POETRY~ A Daybook
Translation & Introduction by Paul Smith
This is a Daybook of Sufi and Dervish Poetry in the *Ruba'i* form, from the Arabic, Persian, Turkish & Urdu from Rudaki to Modern Times. 366 inspirational and spiritually helpful and beautiful poems by the greatest Sufi poets of all time including Rudaki, Mansur Hallaj, Shibli, Baba Tahir, Abu Said, Ibn Sina, Baba Kuhi, Ansari, Al-Ghazali, Hamadani, Khayyam, Sana'i, Mahsati, Khaqani, Nizami, Ruzbihan, Baghdadi, 'Attar, Auhad-ud-din Kermani, Kamal ad-din, Hamavi, Baba Afzal, Rumi, Imami, Sadi, 'Iraqi, Humam, Amir Khusrau, Simnani, Ibn Yamin, Khaju, Obeyd Zakani, Emad, Hafiz, Ruh Attar, Kadi Burhan-ud-din, Jahan Khatun, Maghribi, Nesimi, Kasim Anwar, Shah Ni'matullah, Jami, Baba Fighani, Fuzuli, Ghazali, Urfi, Qutub Shah, Haleti, Dara Shikoh, Sarmad, Sa'ib, Makhfi, Bedil, Mushtaq, Sauda, Esrar Dede, Hatif, Mir, Aatish, Zauq, Dabir, Anees, Hali, Shad, Iqbal, Khalili, Rahi, Firaq, Josh, Nurbakhsh, Paul. Sufis & Dervishes, Their Art & Use of Poetry, The Form & Function of the *Ruba'i*. Pages 390.

~*KABIR*~ A Daybook
Translation & Introduction by Paul Smith
'Here are wonderful words of wisdom (*sakhis*/poems) from one of the wisest of the wise. Here are lines of love from a Master of Divine Love, and a human being who has lived as all human beings should live, with compassion, honesty and courage. If you want the Truth, no holds barred, it is here, but as we're told; truth is dangerous! These poems change people. You will not be the same! As Kabir says. "Wake up sleepy head!"' From

the Introduction that includes a Glossary and a Selected Bibliography. 366 wonderful short poems in this Daybook to inspire and enlighten. 382 pages.

~ABU SA'ID & SARMAD~ A Sufi Daybook
Translation & Introduction by Paul Smith
Abu Sa'id (968-1049) was a Perfect Master and a poet who lived in Nishapur and composed only *ruba'is,* over 400 of them. He was a founder of Sufi poetry and a major influence on the *ruba'i* and most poets that followed, especially Sana'i, Nizami, 'Attar, Rumi and Hafiz. Sarmad (d. 1659) was a famous and infamous Persian dervish poet of Jewish and Armenian origin. As a merchant he gathered his wares and travelled to India to sell them. In India he renounced Judaism and adopted Islam: he later renounced it in favour of Hinduism which he finally renounced for Sufism. He was known for exposing and ridiculing the major religions and hypocrisy of his day, but he also wrote beautiful mystical poetry in the form of *rubai's*. He was beheaded in 1659 by Emperor Aurangzeb for his perceived heretical poetry. This Sufi Daybook consists of 366 of their insightful, beautiful & spiritual *ruba'is,* 188 each. Introduction & Bibliography. 390 pages.

~*SADI*~ A Daybook
Translation & Introduction by Paul Smith
Sadi of Shiraz, along with Hafiz, Nizami & Rumi is considered one of the great mystical and romantic poets of Persia. His masterpieces, *The Rose Garden* and *The Bustan* (Orchard) have been a major influence in the East and West for the past 700 years. His *Divan* of *ghazals* are still much loved. His *ruba'is* have also been an influence on the poets that followed him. Here is a Daybook with a selection of 366 poems from his *ghazals, ruba'is* and *masnavis.* Introduction includes his Life and Times and Poetry. There is also a Selected Bibliography. The correct rhyme-structure has been kept as well as the beauty and meaning of these beautiful, inspirational and spiritual poems. A Daybook to remember each day. 394 pages.

NIZAMI, KHAYYAM & 'IRAQI ... A Daybook
Translation & Introduction by Paul Smith
Here is a unique Daybook of 366 poems by three of Persia's greatest mystical & philosophical poets. Nizami was a true Master Poet who is most famous for his six books in *masnavi* form: *The Treasury of the Mysteries, Khrosrau and Shirin, Layla and Majnun, The Seven Portraits* (another Sufi classic) and his two books on Alexander. He also composed a *Divan* of approximately 20,000 couplets in *ghazals* and *ruba'is* and other

forms... tragically only 200 couplets survive. His influence on 'Attar, Rumi, Sadi, Hafiz and Jami and all others that followed cannot be overestimated. Omar Khayyam was more famous in Persia as an astronomer, philosopher and mathematician... the hedonistic and occasionally Sufi philosophy in his *ruba'is* meant that his poems were never really popular in his homeland, but of course after the work of FitzGerald the west fell in love with him. He stated, "The only group which may reach God with purification of soul and renunciation of sensual preoccupations, with yearning and ecstasy, are the Sufis." 'Iraqi was the author of a *Divan* of spiritual *ghazals* and *ruba'is* and other poems and of the famous work in prose and poetry *Lama'at,* 'Divine Flashes'... a work that beautifully describes the mysteries of Divine Union that became a classic of Sufi Mysticism. The correct rhyme structure has been kept. 380 pages.

~ABU SA'ID & SARMAD~ A Sufi Daybook
Translation & Introduction by Paul Smith
Abu Sa'id (968-1049) was a Perfect Master and a poet who lived in Nishapur and composed only *ruba'is,* over 400 of them. He was a founder of Sufi poetry and a major influence on the *ruba'i* and most poets that followed, especially Sana'i, Nizami, 'Attar, Rumi and Hafiz. Sarmad (d. 1659) was a famous and infamous Persian dervish poet of Jewish and Armenian origin. As a merchant he gathered his wares and travelled to India to sell them. In India he renounced Judaism and adopted Islam: he later renounced it in favour of Hinduism which he finally renounced for Sufism. He was known for exposing and ridiculing the major religions and hypocrisy of his day, but he also wrote beautiful mystical poetry in the form of *rubai's*. He was beheaded in 1659 by Emperor Aurangzeb for his perceived heretical poetry. This Sufi Daybook consists of 366 of their insightful, beautiful & spiritual *ruba'is,* 188 each. Introduction & Bibliography. 390 pages.

ARABIC & AFGHAN SUFI POETRY ... A Daybook
Translation & Introduction by Paul Smith
Here is an enlightened Daybook of 366 inspirational poems by the greatest Arabic & Afghan Sufi poets of all time in the forms of the *ruba'i, ghazal* and others. THE POETS: ARABIC POETS: Hazrat Ali, Ali Ibn Husain, Rabi'a of Basra, Abu Nuwas, Dhu'l-Nun, Bayazid Bistami, Al Nuri, Junaid, Sumnun, Mansur al-Hallaj, Ibn 'Ata, Shibli, Ibn Sina, Al-Ghazzali, Gilani, Abu Madyam, Suhrawadi, Ibn al-Farid, Ibn 'Arabi, Al-Busiri, Al-Shushtari, Ahmed Shawqi. AFGHAN POETS: Mirza, Khushal, Ashraf Khan, Bedil, Abdul-Kadir, Rahman Baba, Khwaja

Mohammad, Hamid, Ahmad Shah, Shaida, Khalili. The correct form and meaning has been kept in all of these spiritual poems. Introduction on the Spiritual meaning of Sufi poetry and its various forms. 392 pages.

TURKISH & URDU SUFI POETS...
A Daybook
Translation & Introduction by Paul Smith
Here is an enlightened Daybook of 366 inspirational poems by the greatest Turkish & Urdu Sufi poets of all time in the forms of the *ruba'i, ghazal* and others. THE POETS: Turkish... Ahmed Yesevi, Sultan Valad, Yunus Emre, Kadi Burhan-ud-din, Nesimi, Ahmedi, Suleyman Chelebi, Sheykhi, Necati, Zati, Pir Sultan, Khayali, Fuzuli, Baqi, Huda'i, Nef'i, Yahya, Haleti, Na'ili, Niyazi, Galib, Esrar Dede, Leyla Khanim, Veysel. Urdu... Qutub Shah, Wali, Sauda, Dard, Nazir, Mir, Aatish, Zafar, Zauq, Momin, Dabir, Anees, Hali, Shad, Inayat Khan, Iqbal, Asghar, Jigar. The correct form and meaning has been kept in all of these spiritual poems. Introduction on Turkish, Urdu Poetry and the Spiritual meaning of Sufi poetry. 394 pages.

SUFI & DERVISH RUBA'IYAT (9th – 14th century)
~ A Daybook~
Translation & Introduction by Paul Smith
Here is an enlightened Daybook of 366 inspirational poems in the form of the *ruba'i* by the greatest Sufi & Dervish poets and Spiritual Masters from the 9th to the 14th century. THE POETS: Rudaki, Mansur al-Hallaj, Shibli, Baba Tahir, Abu Said, Ibn Sina, Baba Kuhi, Ansari, Al-Ghazali, Hamadani, Omar Khayyam, Sana'i, Mahsati, Khaqani, Nizami, Ruzbihan, Baghdadi, 'Attar, Auhad-ud-din Kermani, Kamal ad-din, Hamavi, Baba Afzal, Rumi, Imami, Sadi, 'Iraqi, Sultan Valad, Humam, Amir Khusrau, Simnani, Ibn Yamin, Khaju, Obeyd Zakani, Emad, Hafiz. Introduction is on Sufi Poetry and on the form & function of the *ruba'i*. 394 pages.

SUFI & DERVISH RUBA'IYAT (14th[th] – 20th century)
~ A Daybook~
Translation & Introduction by Paul Smith
Here is an enlightened Daybook of 366 inspirational poems in the form of the *ruba'i* by the greatest Sufi & Dervish poets and Spiritual Masters from the 14th to the 20th century. THE POETS: Hafiz, Ruh Attar, Kadi Burhan-ud-din, Jahan Khatun, Kamal, Maghribi, Nesimi, Kasim Anwar, Shah Ni'matullah, Jami, Baba Fighani, Fuzuli, Ghazali, Urfi, Qutub Shah,

Haleti, Dara Shikoh, Sarmad, Sa'ib, Nasir Ali, Makhfi, Bedil, Mushtaq, Sauda, Dard, Esrar Dede, Hatif, Mir, Aatish, Zauq, Dabir, Anees, Hali, Shad, Iqbal, Mehroom, Khalili, Nurbakhsh, Paul. Introduction is on Sufi Poetry and on the form & function of the *ruba'i*. 394 pages.

ABU NUWAS Selected Poems
Translation & Introduction by Paul Smith
Abu Nuwas (757-814) was the most famous and infamous poet who composed in Arabic of the Abbasid era. His style was extravagant and his compositions reflected the licentious manners of the upper classes of his day. His father was Arab and his mother was Persian. As a youth he was sold into slavery; a wealthy benefactor later set him free. By the time he reached manhood he had settled in Baghdad and was composing poetry. It was at this time, because of his long hair, he acquired the name Abu Nuwas (Father of Ringlets). Gradually he attracted the attention of Harun al-Rashid and was given quarters at court. His ability as a poet no doubt was one reason for Abu Nuwas' success with the caliph, but after a while he became known as a reprobate and participated in less reputable pastimes with the ruler. He spent time in Egypt but soon returned to Baghdad to live out his remaining years. It is said he lived the last part of his life as a Sufi and some of his poems reflect this. He is popular today, perhaps more so than he ever was, as a kind of comic anti-hero in many Muslim countries. His poems consist of *qit'as* (of which he was the first master) *ghazals* and *qasidas*. His poems could be classified into: praises (of nobles and caliphs & famous people), mockeries, jokes, complaints, love of men and women, wine, hunting, laments, asceticism. All forms are here in the true meaning & rhyme structure. Introduction on his Life, Times & Poetry and forms he composed in and an Appendix of some of the stories about him in the Arabian Nights. 154 pages.

~*NAZIR AKBARABADI*~ Selected Poems
Translation and Introduction Paul Smith
Nazir Akbarabadi (1735-1830) is an Indian poet known as the 'Father of *Nazm*', who wrote mainly Urdu *ghazals* and *nazms*. It is said that Nazir's poetic treasure consisted of about 200,000 but only about 6000 couplets remain. The canvas of Nazir's *nazms* is so vast that it encompasses all aspects of human behavior and every person can find *nazms* that can suit his taste. Many of his poems are about daily life and observations of things such as training a young bear or the pleasures of the rainy season, how beauty can fade, the lives of old prostitutes, etc. His poems are loved by folk today. Many of his poems are spiritual and he is seen as a true Sufi. Bankey

Behari: 'He saw the Lord everywhere. His meditations led him to the realization of the Forms of the Lord as well as the Formless Divinity. He sings of Shri Krishna with the greatest fervour as of Hazrat Ali and the Prophet Mohammed, and turns his face if he comes across the pseudo-saints and religious preceptors who are wanting in realization and yet profess it. By far he is best in portraying the heat of his yearning for his vision.' This is the largest translation of his poetry into English, with the correct form & meaning. Introduction on his Life, Times & Poetry and on the poetic forms he used. Selected Bibliography. 191 pages.

GREAT SUFI POETS OF THE PUNJAB & SINDH: AN ANTHOLOGY
Translations, Introductions by Paul Smith

The ideal of the Punjabi & Sindhi Sufi poets was to find God in all His creation and thus attain union with Him. Thus union or annihilation in God was to be fully achieved after death, but in some cases it was gained while living. This Sufi poetry consequently is full of poems, songs, and hymns praising the Beloved, describing the pain and sorrow inflicted by separation, and ultimately the joy, peace and knowledge attained in the union. CONTENTS: Introduction: Sufis & Dervishes: Their Art and Use of Poetry... 7, Sufi Poets of the Punjab... 33, Sufi Poets of Sindh...37 THE POETS... Baba Farid... 41, Sultan Bahu... 69, Bulleh Shah... 85, Ali Haider... 113, Farid... 123, Shah Latif... 133, Sachal Sarmast... 155. The correct rhyme-structure and spiritual meaning has been kept in these beautiful, spiritual & inspiring poems. 166 pages.

~RUBA'IYAT OF IQBAL~
Translation & Introduction by Paul Smith

Muhammad Iqbal (1873-1938) was born in Sialkot, Punjab. He graduated from Government College, Lahore with a master's degree in philosophy. He taught there while he established his reputation as an Urdu poet. During this period his poetry expressed an ardent Indian nationalism, but a marked change came over his views when he was studying for his doctorate at Cambridge, visiting German universities and qualifying as a barrister. The philosophies of Nietzsche and Bergson influenced him and he became critical of Western civilization that he regarded as decadent. He turned to Islam and Sufism for inspiration and rejected nationalism as a disease of the West. These ideas found expression in his long poems written in Persian, presumably to gain his ideas an audience in the Moslem world outside India. Becoming convinced that Muslims were in danger from the Hindu majority if India should become independent, he gave his support to

Jinnah as the leader of India's Muslims. He is perhaps the last great master of the famous four-line *ruba'i* form of poetry, having composed over 550 of them in Persian & Urdu. Here is the largest collection of his *ruba'is* in English in book form, in the correct rhyme-structure and meaning. Introduction on his life, times & poetry and the form, function & history of the *ruba'i*. Bibliography. 175 pages.

~*IQBAL*~ SELECTED POETRY
Translation & Introduction by Paul Smith
Muhammad Iqbal (1873-1938) was born in Sialkot, Punjab. He graduated from Government College, Lahore with a master's degree in philosophy. He taught there while he established his reputation as an Urdu poet. During this period his poetry expressed an ardent Indian nationalism, but a marked change came over his views when he was studying for his doctorate at Cambridge, visiting German universities and qualifying as a barrister. The philosophies of Nietzsche and Bergson influenced him and he became critical of Western civilization that he regarded as decadent. He turned to Islam and Sufism for inspiration and rejected nationalism as a disease of the West. These ideas found expression in his long poems written in Persian, presumably to gain his ideas an audience in the Moslem world outside India. Becoming convinced that Muslims were in danger from the Hindu majority if India should become independent, he gave his support to Jinnah as the leader of India's Muslims. In his final years he returned to Urdu as his medium with *ghazals* inspired by his on-and-off Sufism. Here is the largest collection of his poems in English in book form, in the correct rhyme-structure and meaning. Introduction on his life, times & poetry and the forms he wrote in. 183 pages.

>THE POETRY OF INDIA<
Anthology of Poets of India from 3500 B.C. to the 20th century
Translations, Introductions... Paul Smith
India has a great tradition of poetry over the past 5,500 years. From the *Ramayana* of Valmiki through to the *Bhakti* and Sufi poets and those of the recent past, its poetry is surely unique. Here for the first time is the largest anthology of all India's greatest poets, poems in the correct rhyme-structure and meaning to be studied and loved in all their beauty and spiritual significance. Here are over 100 of India's greatest poets, many of them women, including... Valmiki, Vyasa, Kalidasa, Appar, Andal, Mas'ud Sa'd, Jayadeva, Mu'in, Baba Farid, Amir Khusrau, Hasan Dihlavi, Jana Bai, Namdev, Dnyaneshwar, Lalla Ded, Vidyapati, Chandidas, Kabir, Nanak, Surdas, Babur, Mira Bai, Ghazali, Tulsidas, Eknath, Akbar,

Dadu, Rasakhan, Urfi, Naziri, Qutub Shah, Sa'ib, Kalim, Dara Shikoh, Sarmad, Tukaram, Sultan Bahu, Nasir Ali, Ramdas, Bahina Bai, Makhfi, Vemana, Wali, Bedil, Bulleh Shah, Shah Latif, Ali Haider, Sauda, Dard, Nazir, Mir, Sachal Sarmast, Aatish, Zauq, Ghalib, Dabir, Anees, Shefta, Henry Derozio, Dagh, Farid, Shad, Tagore, Iqbal, Puran Singh, Inayat Khan, Jigar, Huma. Introduction on The Main Forms in the Poetry of India. Pages... 622.

BHAKTI POETRY OF INDIA
An Anthology
Translations & Introductions Paul Smith

Bhakti is the love felt by the worshipper towards the personal God. While *bhakti* as designating a religious path is already a central concept in the *Bhagavad Gita,* it rises to importance in the medieval history of Hinduism, where the *Bhakti Movement* saw a rapid growth of *bhakti* beginning in Southern India with the Vaisnava Alvars (6th-9th century) and Saiva Nayanars (5th-10th century), who spread *bhakti* poetry and devotion throughout India by the 12th-18th century. The *Bhakti* movement reached North India in the Delhi Sultanate. After their encounter with the expanding religion of Islam and especially Sufism, *bhakti* proponents, who were traditionally called 'saints,' encouraged individuals to seek personal union with the divine. Its influence also spread to other religions. THE POETS: Appar, Andal, Jayadeva, Janabai, Namdev, Dnaneshwar, Lalla Ded, Vidyapati, Chandidas, Kabir, Nanak, Surdas, Mira Bai, Tulsidas, Eknath, Dadu, Rasakhan, Tukaram, Ramdas, Bahina Bai. Introduction on *Bhakti* & the *Bhakti* Poets of India & The Main Forms in the *Bhakti* Poetry of India. The correct rhyme-structure and meaning is here in these poems. Pages 236.

SAYINGS OF KRISHNA
A DAYBOOK
Translation & Introduction Paul Smith

These 366 wise, powerful, loving, enlightened and still totally relevant saying are from the *Bhagavad Gita,* a 700-verse Hindu scripture that is part of the ancient Sanskrit epic, the *Mahabharata,* but is frequently treated as a freestanding text, and in particular as an *Upanishad* in its own right, one of the several books that constitute general Vedic tradition. It is revealed scripture in the views of Hindus, the scripture for Hindus represents the words and message of God, the book is considered among the most important texts in the history of literature and philosophy. The teacher of the *Bhagavad Gita* is Lord Krishna, who is revered by Hindus as a manifestation of God (Parabrahman) Himself, and is referred to as Bhagavan, the Divine One. His sayings are in answers to questions asked by Arjuna, a disciple, on the eve of a battle. "I have revealed to you the Truth, the Mystery of mysteries. Having thought it over, you are free to act as you will." Pages 376.

~CLASSIC POETRY OF AZERBAIJAN~
~An Anthology~
Translation & Introduction Paul Smith
Here is one of the few anthologies in English of the greatest poets of Azerbaijan in the classic period, from the 11th to the 17th century. All the poems translated here in the forms of the *ghazal, masnavi, ruba'i, qit'a* and *qasida* have been kept to the correct rhyme and meaning. The poets are… Qatran, Mahsati, Mujir, Khaqani, Nizami, Shabistari, Humam, Kadi Buran-ud-din, Nasim Anwar, Nesimi, Khata'i, Fuzuli and Sa'ib. There is an Introduction on Various Forms in the Classical Poetry of Azerbaijan and biographies and further reading options on all of these always engrossing and powerful, beautiful, mysterious, often romantic and spiritual and often Sufi poets. Included is the female poet Mahsati, one of the greatest poets of the east and Nizami, one of the greatest poets of all time. 231 pages.

MANSUR HALLAJ: THE TAWASIN
(Book of the Purity of the Glory of the One)
Translation & Introduction Paul Smith
The Perfect Master, poet & martyr, Husayn Mansur al-Hallaj (died 919), was born near Shiraz and was tortured and executed in Baghdad for declaring: "I am the Truth *(Anal Haq)."* Much has been written about his famous (and infamous) statement and his masterpiece *The Tawasin* in which he makes it. 'Written in rhymed Arabic prose… it sets forth a doctrine of saintship—a doctrine founded on personal experience and clothed in the form of a subtle yet passionate dialectic.' R.A. Nicholson. The Introduction here contains: The Life, Times and Works of Mansur Hallaj, The Perfect Master *(Qutub),* 'Anal-Haq' or 'I am the Truth' of Mansur Hallaj, Four Master Poets of Baghdad who influenced Hallaj and A Selection of Poetry from the Persian, Turkish, Pushtu & Urdu Poets about or influenced by Mansur Hallaj. Appendix: The Story of Idris (Azazil) and Adam From *'The Book of Genesis'* of Shahin of Shiraz. This is a free-form poetic translation that captures the beauty, meaning, profundity of this classic of Sufism. Pages 264.

MOHAMMED
In Arabic, Sufi & Eastern Poetry
Translation & Introduction by Paul Smith
Here is a collection of poems from the time of Prophet Mohammed in the 7th century into the 20th century about him and in praise of him by some of the greatest poets writing in Arabic, Persian, Turkish and Urdu of all time, most of them Sufis. The *Koran* itself like the books of most great Spiritual Masters was in poetry as were the sayings of Jesus, Krishna, Rama, Zarathustra. There is an Introduction on Prophecy & Poetry and on the various forms of poetry used by the poets in this anthology. Included in this anthology are complete translations of the famous three *Qasidas of the Prophet's Mantle*. THE POETS (in order of appearance): Ka'b ibn Zuhair, Firdausi, Baba Kuhi, Abu Maydan, Nizami, Mu'inuddin Chishti, Ibn 'Arabi, Rumi, Al-Busiri, Sadi, Shabistari, Yunus Emre, Hafiz, Nesimi, Suleyman Chelibi, Shah Ni'matu'llah, Makhfi, Hayati, Aatish, Iqbal, Ahmed Shawqi. Pages 245.

GITA GOVINDA
The Dance of Divine Love of Radha & Krishna
>Jayadeva<
Translation by Puran Singh & Paul Smith
Jayadeva (circa 1200 AD.) was a Sanskrit poet and most known for his immortal composition, the epic poem/play *Gita Govinda* that depicts the divine love of Avatar Krishna and his consort, Radha. This poem is considered an important text in the Bhakti (Path of Love) movement of Hinduism. The work delineates the love of Krishna for Radha, the milkmaid, his faithlessness and subsequent return to her, and is taken as symbolical of the human soul's straying from its true allegiance but returning at length to the God that created it. It elaborates the eight moods of the heroine that over the years has been an inspiration for many paintings, compositions and choreographic works in Indian classical dances. It has been translated to many languages and is considered to be among the finest examples of Sanskrit poetry. Paul Smith has worked with Puran Singh's powerful & beautiful original free-form poetic version and brought it up to date. Introduction on Life & Times & Poetry of Kayadeva. Glossary. Pages 107.

THE BHAGAVAD GITA: The Gospel of the Lord Shri Krishna
Translated from original Sanskrit with Introduction by Shri Purohit Swami
General Introductions and to Chapters by Charles Johnston
Revised into Modern English with an Introduction by Paul Smith

The Bhagavad Gita is the single most famous poem in the ancient literature of India. It is equally celebrated as the highest spiritual philosophy and poetry. It constitutes the beginning and in a sense the end of any true knowledge of Indian mysticism. The translator refers to it as 'The Bible of India'. The Guardian said of this translation in 1935 when it was first published: "A beautiful rendering, and gives the reader a clearer and more truthful impression of what the Indian reader takes it to mean than a literal translation would do." Illustrated. 326 pages.

THE DHAMMAPADA: The Gospel of the Buddha
Revised Version by Paul Smith
from translation from the Pali of F. Max Muller
From ancient times to now, the Dhammapada has been regarded as the most succinct expression of the Buddha's teaching and the chief spiritual testament of early Buddhism. In the countries following Buddhism, the influence of the Dhammapada is immeasurable. It is a guidebook for resolving problems of everyday life, and a primer for the instruction in the wisdom of understanding. The admiration the Dhammapada has elicited has not been confined to followers of Buddhism. Wherever it has become known, its moral earnestness, realistic understanding of human life, wisdom and stirring message of a way to freedom from suffering have won for it the devotion and veneration of those responsive to the good and the true. 247 pages

'IRAQI: SELECTED POEMS
Translation & Introduction by Paul Smith
'Iraqi (1213-1289) was the author of a *Divan* of spiritual *ghazals* and *ruba'is* and the famous work in prose and poetry… *Lama'at,* 'Divine Flashes'… a classic of Sufi Mysticism. He was born in Hamadan in western Persia and as a child learnt the *Koran* by heart. He travelled from Persia to India with dervishes where he stayed for 25 years. It is said that on his travels he met Rumi. His grave is in Damascus beside that of another great Perfect Master and poet Ibn al-'Arabi. When seeing these graves a pilgrim stated, "That ('Iraqi) is the Persian Gulf and this (Ibn al- 'Arabi) is the Arabian Sea." Introduction: The Life & Times & Poems of 'Iraqi, Selected Bibliography, Forms in Classical Persian Poetry Used by 'Iraqi. *Rubai's, Ghazals, Qasida, Masnavis, Tarji-band*. The correct rhyme-structure has been kept as well as the beauty and meaning of these beautiful, mystical poems. 158 pages.

ZARATHUSHTRA: SELECTED POEMS
A New Verse Translation and Introduction by Paul Smith from the Original Translation by D.J. Irani. Original Introduction by Rabindranath Tagore.
The Perfect Master and Prophet and one of the first poets Zarathushtra (Zoroaster) lived approx. 7000 B.C. and through his teaching of 'Good words, good thoughts, good deeds' brought in his poems that are similar in form to *ruba'is* a revelation and dispensation of Divinity. His teaching and poetry have influenced most religions that followed and his poems/songs were a great influence on many of the Sufi poets, including Rumi. Here are 116 of his profound, simple, inspiring poems selected from the *Gathas*. 141 pages.

THE YOGA SUTRAS OF PATANJALI
"The Book of the Spiritual Man" An Interpretation By Charles Johnston
General Introduction by Paul Smith
The Yoga Sutras of Patanjali are 194 Indian *sutras* (aphorisms) that constitute the foundational text of Raja Yoga. Yoga is one of the six orthodox schools of Hindu philosophy. Various authorities attribute the compilation to Patanjali 2nd century BCE. In the Yoga Sutras, Patanjali prescribes adherence to eight 'limbs' or steps to quiet one's mind and liberation. The Sutras not only provide yoga with a thorough and consistent philosophical basis, they also clarify many important esoteric concepts that are common to all traditions of Indian thought, such as *karma*. Pages 173

POETRY

THE MASTER, THE MUSE & THE POET
An Autobiography in Poetry by... Paul Smith
Born in Melbourne, Australia, in 1945, Paul Smith began composing poems in the ancient Persian form of the *ghazal* at the age of 6 on his way to school. Here are most of his poems composed over the past 45 years... free-form, rhyming, *ruba'is, ghazals, masnavis* etc. Here are poems composed at home or travelling in the East and the U.S.A while giving readings of his poetry and translations. Here are poems of a personal nature, about human love & grief, about evolution and God and man and the environment and the past, present and future. Many of the poems were composed while translating the works of Hafiz, Sadi, Nizami, Rumi, Kabir, Obeyd Zakani, Jahan Khutan and many others and while writing novels, screenplays and plays where he continued to tell the inner and outer story of his passage

through this mysterious and wonderful and sometimes very painful life. 637 Pages.

PUNE: THE CITY OF GOD
(A Spiritual Guidebook to the New Bethlehem)
Poems & Photographs in Praise of Avatar Meher Baba by Paul Smith
In 1985 the author began to feel the need (usually on the site, or shortly afterwards) to put pen to paper and express in free-form, internally-rhyming poetry… a kind of descriptive inner and outer guide to each 'Baba place' in Meher Baba's birth-place of Pune, as he was experiencing it… a 'feeling' of the presence of the Master from the past that was *still available*… and, (having gone back often to many of the places and discovered this)… *the future*. He began to take photographs of the places at the same time, sometimes even in the middle of writing the poem. Interestingly, often when he read these poems to others they inspired them to visit Pune and see and experience Meher Baba's presence in these places for themselves. 159 pages.

COMPASSIONATE ROSE
Recent Ghazals for Avatar Meher Baba
by Paul Smith
While working on the *ghazals* of Hafiz and Sadi, Jahan Khatun, Nizami, Obeyd Zakani and many other Persian, Urdu, Turkish & Pushtu Poets for 40 years the author often composed *ghazals* inspired by his Spiritual Master Meher Baba. His earliest *ghazals* plus other poems inspired by him were published in the volume 'A Bird in His Hand'. The *ghazals* in this volume were composed while in India staying with Meher Baba's nephews Sohrab & Rustom Irani in Pune in 2004 and on return to Australia over the following two years under difficult health conditions. They are published here in the sequence in which they were written. 88 pages.

~THE ULTIMATE PIRATE~ (and the Shanghai of Imagination)
A FABLE
by Paul Smith
This long poem and the poems related to it were composed in 1973 while translating '*Divan* of Hafiz'. The author had read Meher Baba's masterpiece 'God Speaks' that explained everything and in particular, the inner planes of consciousness… of which this is an imagined fable about such a journey. His 'Creative Imagination' at the time was so acute and deep that the journey at times seemed so real that he passed out from the bliss that he was experiencing. Since a child he had always loved pirate movies and to a certain extent in this poem he pays homage to them through

the Ultimate Pirate, this time, his Spiritual Master, Meher Baba. Illustrations by Oswald Hall. 157 pages.

+THE CROSS OF GOD+
A Poem in the *Masnavi* Form
by Paul Smith

The *masnavi* is the form used in Persian, Turkish, Urdu and other poetry to write epic ballads or romances and is essentially a Persian invention. Each couplet has a different rhyme with both lines rhyming. This is to allow the poet greater freedom to go into a longer description of the subject he has chosen to present. All of the great, long, narrative poems of Persia were composed in this form that is not known in classical Arabic poetry. The most famous poems written in this form are the 'Shahnama' (Book of the Kings) of Firdausi, the 'Enclosed Garden of the Truth' of Sana'i, the 'Five Treasures' of Nizami, the 'Conference of the Birds' and 'The Book of God' and many others by 'Attar, the 'Seven Thrones' of Jami, the ten *masnavis* of Amir Khusraw and of course the great '*Masnavi*' of Rumi. Here is a *masnavi* by poet and translator Paul Smith based on the following from Isaiah 53: "It is certain, the cross could not have existed without the efforts of Jesus, who is responsible for the tree, the nails & the tools that fashioned the cross; as well as the materials that fashioned the scourge, which caused His suffering."

It explores with much beauty and insight the relationship between an extraordinary father and son and one's spiritual responsibility. It is a long poem for the purity inside of each of us. (7x10 inches).

CRADLE MOUNTAIN
Paul Smith… Illustrations – John Adam

In 1970 an Australian poet, Paul Smith, read in a newspaper of the death of a young fellow-poet on Cradle Mountain in Tasmania. He was deeply touched by the young man's fate and immediately began writing a poem in praise of the poet, Stephen Baxter. He contacted a friend, the artist John Adam, who read his poem and was inspired enough to illustrate it. The book was published in a limited edition to good reviews and quickly sold out. Stephen Baxter's family contacted him and told him he had truly captured the life and unfortunate death of the young poet. This newly revised edition is close to that of the original and contains all of John Adam's inspired illustrations. (7x10 inches) Second Edition.

RUBA'IYAT ~ of ~ PAUL SMITH
The *ruba'i* is an ancient form of poetry of four lines in which usually the first, second and fourth lines rhyme and sometimes with the *radif* (refrain) after the rhyme words... sometimes all four rhyme. Each *ruba'i* is a separate poem in itself. The *ruba'i* should be eloquent, spontaneous and ingenious. Every major and most minor poet of Persia and Turkey and India composed at some times in the *ruba'i* form. Paul Smith, an Australian poet, has translated all the major Sufi and other poets of this form and has composed many of his own in English over the past 45 years. Here is a large selection of his work that is at once modern and reflecting all the great Sufi *ruba'i* poets of the past. The Introduction includes chapters on his life and work, Sufism in poetry and a chapter on this popular form. Selected Bibliography. Pages 236.

FICTION

THE FIRST MYSTERY.
A Novel of the Road...
by Paul Smith
THE FIRST MYSTERY is a novel that operates on a number of levels: it is a search, a tracking down of a murderer and a mystery as to who did it. It is a search through many mysterious lands, people and events. Travel Australia, Singapore, Malaysia, Thailand, Cambodia, Laos, Burma, Nepal, Tibet, Kashmir, India and San Francisco. It is a search (through dreams and visions) into the sub-conscious mind of the private detective Dave, representing the cynical westerner, who seeks but is unaware of the true nature of his journey. It is also the story of the other main characters, Johnny Wilkulda an Australian aboriginal tracker who represents the intuitive side of humankind, seeking a higher truth for himself and all others; and Robinson, the 'LSD Professor', who has taken the road of mind-expanding drugs, the 'fast road'. Meet Evie Rush, too beautiful to be a murderer? Meet Collins the murderous homicide detective; meet Arla, the beautiful jazz singer in big trouble in Bangkok; meet Margaret, haunted, looking for love in a rubber plantation in Malaysia; meet the Cambodian Prince in love with music, trying to stop war entering his country; meet Meera the Indian girl, stuck in a whorehouse in Laos and seeing visions of a new Messiah. Meet them and many other strange and fabulous, weird and wonderful characters in THE FIRST MYSTERY, a new kind of novel. 541 pages

~THE HEALER AND THE EMPEROR~
A Historical Novel Based on a True Story
by Paul Smith

Monsieur Ferrier, lifelong friend of extraordinary poet, composer, linguist, author, mystic and healer… Fabre D'Olivet stands at his gravesite. Ferrier remembers Fabre's strange encounter with the unforgettable Chrisna, *Le Revolution* and the influence of libertines Sigault and his sister Amelie until the destinies of the future healer and emperor collide in 1800 when Napoleon seizes power and Fabre criticises him. After a bizarre assassination attempt Napoleon imprisons him. Before imprisonment Fabre has met his 'muse', the beautiful and mysterious Julie Marcel. Napoleon has married *his* muse… the older, cold-hearted and envious Josephine, 'The *only* muse in France'. After conquering most esoteric sciences and languages including the extinct ancient Hebrew, Fabre pens among many other unique works his masterpiece *The Hebraic Tongue Restored and The True Translation of Genesis*. But, to get published in 1811 he has to confront his old nemesis, Napoleon. He must prove the miraculous nature of his discovery of the essence of sound and language. He convinces a congenital deaf-mute's mother to let him try to heal him and after four days is successful! A miracle! Napoleon has him arrested after he cures another and the conflict between the healer and the emperor resumes. This time the lives and hearing of many others are at stake in this novel of an extraordinary true story! Pages 149.

>>>GOING<<<BACK…
A Novel by Paul Smith

GOING BACK is a novel inspired by a true story of love, courage and determination set in a land at peace, Australia; and a land at war… Cambodia. It is the story of people made into refugees by war: the orphans, the old, the young and those who have lost everything and the effect that deadly landmines often have on them. It is the story of the few from America and Australia who stand up to help and love and befriend and help them. But it is mostly the amazing true story of one man who rises out of the depth of despair and through a stroke of good fortune sets off on an odyssey into a living hell and by his inventiveness and sense of humour many lives are saved and changed. Unlike other stories set in Vietnam and Cambodia that tell of war from the soldiers point of view, GOING BACK tells the tale of an ordinary man and people who act extraordinarily in the worst kinds of situations. It is a story from the recent past that could have been ripped from the headlines of today and probably tomorrow. It is an important story, a sad, funny, weird, fantastic, awful, heroic story of war and love and peace and friendship that has to be told. 164 pages.

CHILDREN'S FICTION

PAN OF THE NEVER-NEVER
by Paul Smith

Pan is awoken, after sleeping for over a 100 years, in the great wilderness of Wilson's Promontory, Australia (the real Never-Never Land) by a police helicopter searching for Brad Becker, escaped from a children's home outside Wonthaggi, operated by the abusive Mr. Harvey. Pan meets Brad who can't believe who he is but after a fast flight changes his mind. Pan needs help to dig out the lost boys old hide-out. While Brad snoozes, Pan flies over the area to check on the changes while he slept and is happy to have an encounter with the 'Pirates' motorcycle gang unloading drugs from a yacht. Pan flies Brad by night to the Children's Home to bring back Brad's friends … a new lot of 'lost boys'. But there's a snag in the guise of Sandy and Kym. Girls! The other gang members are little Danny who has discovered who Pan really is, Greg, the tractor driver; Mario, an Italian kid and Ben, an Aborigine who amazingly converses with Pan in his mother tongue. Pan flies Sandy down to check out the yacht and search for the 'Pirates' but Pan and Sandy are outsmarted and find themselves all tied up ready to become the sharks breakfast! The others break through to the "lost boys" old hide-out! They discover Pan's strange diary and flashes of his life over 2340 years open up to them as the adventure continues… but, where are Pan and Sandy? 126 pages.

~HAFIZ~
The Ugly Little Boy who became a Great Poet
by Paul Smith

HAFIZ is the true story of the ugliest boy of his age but with a remarkable memory whose father dies when he is eight and he has to live with his mother at his Uncle Sadi's house. Hafiz goes to work in a drapery shop where he becomes part of the people's overthrowing of a cruel ruler. He then becomes an apprentice baker, who delivers bread to the rich suburbs of Shiraz, Persia in 1320. One day he catches sight of Nabat, the beautiful daughter of one of the cities wealthy traders, promised to a handsome prince. Hafiz pours his love into his poems/songs dedicated to her. His words are so wondrous that the greatest minstrel of the day Hajji, takes up his instrument and serenades his loved one for him. His experiences with his Spiritual Master, Attar, and his songs and poems soon establish Hafiz as a force for truth and beauty through his much loved Shiraz, ravaged by wars and revolutions. Fame doesn't come easily as the ruthless rulers and priests conspire to silence the ever-increasing power of Hafiz's voice. Will he and Nabat and his friends like the jester Obeyd and the minstrel Hajji survive? Can words of love defeat hate's sword? Will Hafiz gain his heart's desire? 195 pages.

> "To penetrate into the essence of all being and significance
> and to release the fragrance of that inner attainment
> for the guidance and benefit of others, by expressing
> in the world of forms, truth, love, purity and beauty…
> this is the only game which has any intrinsic and absolute
> worth. All other, happenings, incidents and attainments can,
> in themselves, have no lasting importance."
> Meher Baba

Printed in Great Britain
by Amazon